Assessments and Activities for Teaching Swimming

Monica Lepore
West Chester University

Luis Columna
Syracuse University

Lauren Friedlander Litzner
Montgomery County Public School, Rockville, Maryland

Human Kinetics

Library of Congress Cataloging-in-Publication Data

Lepore, Monica, 1956-
 Assessments and activities for teaching swimming / Monica Lepore, Luis Columna, and Lauren Friedlander Litzner.
     pages cm
 Includes bibliographical references.
 1. Swimming--Study and teaching. 2. Aquatic exercises. 3. Individualized instruction.
I. Columna, Luis. II. Litzner, Lauren Friedlander, 1987- III. Title.
 GV836.35.L47 2015
 797.2'1--dc23

                                        2014003543

ISBN: 978-1-4504-4472-9 (print)

Developmental Editor: Ragen E. Sanner; **Managing Editor:** Karla Walsh; **Associate Managing Editor:** B. Rego; **Copyeditor:** Patsy Fortney; **Permissions Manager:** Dalene Reeder; **Graphic Designer:** Dawn Sills; **Cover Designer:** Keith Blomberg; **Photographs (cover and interior):** Neil Bernstein, © Human Kinetics, unless otherwise noted; **Photo Asset Manager:** Laura Fitch; **Visual Production Assistant:** Joyce Brumfield; **Photo Production Manager:** Jason Allen; **Printer:** Versa Press

We thank Syracuse University for assistance in providing the location for the photo shoot for this book.

Printed in the United States of America   10 9 8 7 6 5 4 3 2 1

The paper in this book is certified under a sustainable forestry program.

Human Kinetics
Website: www.HumanKinetics.com

United States: Human Kinetics
P.O. Box 5076
Champaign, IL 61825-5076
800-747-4457
e-mail: humank@hkusa.com

Canada: Human Kinetics
475 Devonshire Road Unit 100
Windsor, ON N8Y 2L5
800-465-7301 (in Canada only)
e-mail: info@hkcanada.com

Europe: Human Kinetics
107 Bradford Road
Stanningley
Leeds LS28 6AT, United Kingdom
+44 (0) 113 255 5665
e-mail: hk@hkeurope.com

Australia: Human Kinetics
57A Price Avenue
Lower Mitcham, South Australia 5062
08 8372 0999
e-mail: info@hkaustralia.com

New Zealand: Human Kinetics
P.O. Box 80
Torrens Park, South Australia 5062
0800 222 062
e-mail: info@hknewzealand.com

E5886

The authors dedicate this book to the late Dr. Carol Huettig of Texas Woman's University. Her vision and passion for providing services for children with disabilities was truly inspirational. Dr. Huettig's aquatic assessment motivated our desire to create the aquatic activities presented in this book.

Contents

Activity Finder

This table is organized alphabetically by major categories of swimming skills. Each category lists all of the sub-skills and associated activities. Some skills have more than one activity. Skill numbers alert you to the level of a particular sub-skill.

Skill number	Skill description	Activity title	Activity page number
Backstroke			
4.12	Backstroke 12 yards with some out-of-water arm recovery	Broken Fan	144
4.13	Backstroke 12 yards with full out-of-water arm recovery	Who Can? You Can!	144
5.3	Backstroke for 12 yards with above-the-water recovery	Wind Me Up	162
		High Five	162
		Rainbow Backstroke Start	163
5.4	Backstroke for 25 yards with above-the-water recovery	How Straight Can You Swim?	164
		Backstroke Balance	164
		Moving Cargo 1	165
6.3	Backstroke 50 yards	Poker Chip Challenge	180
		High Five Fifty	180
6.4	Backstroke 100 yards	Clean Up the Pool 2	181
		Moving Cargo 2	181
6.12	Backstroke 50 yards using a backstroke flip turn at 25 yards	11 and 1	197
		Log Roll	197
Bobbing			
2.1	Bob in chest-deep water once with instructor's help	I See, You Saw	58
		Rocket Ship 2	59
		Ring Around the Rosie	59
2.2	Bob once holding the gutter or pool edge	Magic Spot	60
		Dolphin Jump	60
		Fun With Tigger	61
2.3	Bob once independently	How High	61
2.4	Bob five consecutive times in chest-deep water independently	Head Start	62
3.1	Bob for 10 seconds in chin-deep water	Measure That 1	92
		10-Second Rush	92
		Bull's-Eye	93

(continued)

(continued)

(continued)

(continued)

(continued)

Acknowledgments

We acknowledge the following professionals for their contributions to this book:

- Dr. Margarita Fernández Vivó, University of Puerto Rico, Mayagüez
- Dr. Kristi Roth, University of Wisconsin, Stevens Point
- Dr. Michael Norris, Syracuse University, New York
- Dr. Michelle Dolphin, Upstate Medical University, New York
- Wilmarie Carlo, Escuela Elemental Urbana, Puerto Rico
- Maria Lepore-Stevens, Delaware Department of the Visually Impaired
- Jessica Lynn Rys, Syracuse University, New York
- Alexis Lynn Partyka, Syracuse University, New York
- Helen Schmid, Syracuse University, New York
- Kristine Ciccone, John Adams High School, New York
- Amy Serr, Glen Cove School District, New York
- Melissa Dobson, Albany, New York
- Jean Pyfer and Texas Woman's University for their permission in utilizing the TWU Adapted Aquatics Assessment

We thank West Chester University of Pennsylvania and the Slater family, Olivia Riehl, Patrick Ray, Dylan Lepore-Schuerenbrand, and Liam Holman for their help with photos.

A special thanks to Joseph Lore and Angela Petrie in the Syracuse University Recreation Department for their assistance with securing facilities for the photo shoot

Our thanks to Syracuse University and to the children and their families who helped with the photos: Angela Ambrogne, Lauren Ashby, Casey Sawyer, Juan Burgos, Ava Dwyer, May Dolphin, Tahjmier Brackett, Aidan Brackett, Claire Macero, Emma Macero, Olivia Vought, Addison Donofrio, Niamh Lacey, Orla Lacey, Amelia Whipps, Will Rufa, Amelia Rufa, Oliver Rufa, Samuel Molinet, Maria Molinet, Annabel Molinet, Allison Nethercott, John Nethercott, and Katie Pfohl.

We would like to thank our families for their encouragement and support.

Introduction

Maria is a 19-year-old college freshman who never learned to swim correctly. She is required to take one fitness and wellness class for her degree and has decided to finally take on the challenge of swimming. Her new Swim for Fitness class includes students at a variety of skill levels and with varying abilities, and the instructor provides activities that include multiple ways in which to participate. Maria is excited to be successful in this class so that she can use lap swimming as a lifetime health and fitness activity.

Jordy, a seven-year-old African-American boy living in Center City Philadelphia, signed up for a camp for children living with sickle cell disease. Because he experiences sickle cell crises in cold conditions and has not yet found a warm pool in which to take swim lessons, he does not know how to swim. On day 1 of camp, Jordy told the swim instructor that he wanted to get tested for the "deep end wristband" and proceeded to enter the water for the swim test. He sank rapidly to the bottom of the 5-foot (1.5 m) section. Fortunately, the swim instructor and lifeguard were right there to scoop Jordy back to the surface. When asked why he thought he could pass the swim test, he replied that he had watched Cullen Jones swimming on TV and thought it looked easy.

Justifying an Aquatic Activity Program

The two preceding scenarios demonstrate the variety of people who do not know how to swim and the types of abilities presented in swim classes. It is imperative that all people, regardless of age, ability, and gender, learn to swim.

Swimming is a recreational, educational, and lifesaving skill. According to the Drowning fact sheet from the World Health Organization (2012), drowning is the third leading cause of death from unintentional injury worldwide. Children, males, those who have seizures, people with autism, and those who live in low- to middle-income countries have the highest rates of drowning. In the United States, drowning is the second leading cause of death in children ages 1 to 14 (Centers for Disease Control and Prevention, 2012c). Although swimming is the second most popular sport in the United States (U.S. Census Bureau, 2010) and one of the top three most popular activities for all ages (Sports & Fitness Industry Association, 2011), many children (57.5 percent of African Americans, 30.9 percent of Caucasians) and adults (about 37 percent) report that they cannot swim or cannot swim well (in the deep end) (Gilchrist, Sacks, & Branche, 2000; Irwin, Irwin, & Ryan, 2009).

Formal swimming lessons can reduce the risk of drowning by as much as 88 percent among children aged one to four years, who are at greatest risk of drowning (Brenner, Taneja, Haynie, et al., 2009; Yang, Nong, Li, et al., 2007). In addition to increasing safety, swimming and aquatic activities can also decrease the risks of obesity, cardiovascular disorder, and type II diabetes (Centers for Disease Control, 2012b). Participating in an aerobic activity such as swimming for two hours and 30 minutes a week has been shown to decrease many risk factors for cardiovascular disease. Swimming is an activity that leads to an increase in health and to an active lifestyle (Chase, Sui, & Blair, 2008). Moreover, people report enjoying water-based exercise more than they do land-based exercise. In general, people can exercise longer in water because of the decreased sense of effort and less joint and muscle pain.

Aquatic activities are fun and popular and have great potential to be life-time activities. For this reason, children should be introduced to them early in physical education classes. A carefully designed aquatic program that includes a pre-assessment, an ongoing review of instruction, and a post-assessment can improve the swimming skills of all individuals, including those with disabilities (Asher, Rivara, Felix, et al., 1995; Huettig & Darden-Melton, 2004; Lepore, Gayle, & Stevens, 2007). Because those with disabilities find many experiences easier in the pool, aquatic programs can improve their overall health and well-being (e.g., aerobic capacity, muscular strength and endurance, and daily living skills) in a way that might not be possible with land-based activities because of the deleterious effects of gravity.

The variety of skill levels found in aquatic education programs often presents challenges to instructors. Because general aquatic activities are not always easily adaptable to those with learning challenges or disabilities, instructors often need more information on how to include such students (Conatser, Block, & Lepore, 2000). This book introduces a variety of aquatic activities in a way that includes students at various ability levels (i.e., a universal design approach). When this universal approach is not broad enough to meet the needs of all students, modifications to the activities are provided.

Safety in Aquatic Programs

All aquatic programs must have an emergency action plan to ensure the safety of all patrons and personnel. Such a plan should include clearly posted rules, a certified lifeguard with no role except to lifeguard, a certified swim instructor from a nationally recognized water safety organization, and a risk management plan. Following are examples of rules that should be posted:

- No running
- No pushing
- No dangerous horseplay
- Dive only on designated areas

In addition, every aquatic program should have appropriate rescue and first aid equipment on hand, such as the following:

- Bandages
- Rescue mask
- Non-latex gloves
- Roller gauze
- Medical tape
- Rescue tube
- Shepherd's crook

Using This Book

Part I includes background information you need to get started. Chapter 1 provides teaching strategies to maximize the aquatic experience for students with and without disabilities. Chapter 2 addresses the importance of conducting an assessment to determine what the student can do and the areas in which the student needs to improve.

The six levels in part II are the meat of this book. They provide 206 activities that are aligned with the six levels of the modified Texas Woman's University (TWU) aquatic assessment, and will make your lessons fun and appropriate for the developmental levels of your students.

Each level begins with an assessment checklist for the skills focused on within the chapter as well as a general description of that level. Skills are organized in the checklist and the sections by similarities. Each skill section within the chapter provides a description of the skill as it is being used for that level of skill and may also include cues and differentiation ideas (or ways to modify the activities). All of the skills in all of the levels follow the same format. Some are repeated in later levels but in more advanced forms. For example, bobbing is introduced in level 2, but is used again in other levels in more advanced activities.

Summary

Aquatic experiences help people of varying ability levels improve their well-being throughout their lifetimes. For these experiences to be positive, certain modifications may be required. When designing your lessons, consider the various needs of your participants, the complexity of the task, and the environmental factors.

The aquatic activities in this book accommodate most students and follow a progression from simple to complex to facilitate both teaching and learning. The purpose of this book is twofold: (1) to provide physical education teachers, camp administrators, recreation specialists, parents, and aquatics professionals with strategies for assessing the present level of performance in an aquatic environment for those with and without disabilities, and (2) to provide aquatic activity suggestions that are aligned with the modified version of the TWU aquatic assessment instrument as shown in this book.

Note: If you use the metric system in your measurements, you can replace any mention of yards with the same number of meters.

PART I

The Art and Science of Teaching Swimming

Part I presents a rationale for providing safe and developmentally appropriate aquatic experiences for students with and without disabilities. This section of the book addresses how to select developmentally appropriate aquatic activities for all learners. In addition, it includes information about the assessment and instruction of basic swimming skills.

Chapter 1 presents strategies for teaching swimming skills based on the concepts of universal design of learning and differentiation of instruction. Chapter 2 highlights the importance of conducting an aquatic assessment before, during, and after the implementation of an aquatic program. You will learn about swim skill assessments that can be used in a variety of aquatic environments.

Strategies for Teaching Everyone

WALK-DO NOT RUN

Coach DJ taught swim lessons every Saturday morning throughout the year to a group of 10 fourth-graders. He enjoyed his level 3 students and came up with many games to teach aquatic activities so that all of his students could experience success. He based his aquatic curriculum on the modified Texas Woman's University (TWU) aquatic assessment levels.

Coach DJ was not stuck in a "my way or the highway" mentality regarding what should be taught and how. He always met his group near the hydraulic lift (a boy in the class who used a wheelchair needed the lift to enter the pool), and he always had a list of the skills and activities his students would be working on that day posted on a large whiteboard near the pool entrance. He was very animated in his demonstrations and was famous for using a beeping kitchen timer so everyone in the group would know how long to stay on task.

Coach DJ's students liked that he offered them many alternatives to choose from for every skill they learned, and that he provided several ways to show mastery of an activity or skill. For example, when the group was learning the kneeling dive, coach DJ crafted a folded mat that anyone could sit on before the dive. For students who were afraid or uncomfortable with the kneeling dive, he placed a mat over the edge of the pool and drenched it with water so students could slide down on their fronts to simulate the movement of the dive. When most of the group had moved on to the actual kneeling dive, the mat helped Kevin, the boy who used a wheelchair, feel more included by giving him some height so he could perform a dive that was closer to a kneeling dive than diving from a seated position at the pool edge. Coach DJ offered the mat to all students in the group, and Kevin and one other student used it during practice.

Coach DJ did not know it, but he was using universal design for learning and differentiation of instruction. These two processes are used in planning and implementing curricula, assessing student learning, and creating lesson plans and activities to meet the needs of students with a wide range of abilities in a general aquatics class.

Coach DJ, like many aquatics instructors, is innovative in his approach and wants to see all of his students learn to swim. Classes like his are common: children with and without disabilities, a multitude of ability levels, and one instructor. Because of the increased diversity in aquatic programs and classes, as well as updates to laws such as the 2010 guidelines for swimming pool accessibility in the Americans with Disabilities Act (a U.S. law mandating accommodations for people with disabilities in all areas of life), instructors must provide reasonable accommodation.

As an aquatics instructor, you will meet children and adults who differ in what motivates them and in their ability to understand directions, attend to tasks, complete practice activities, process information, and enter and exit the aquatic facility. You will need to be creative in coming up with alternative approaches to implementing your aquatic curriculum. Your job will involve assessing your students; providing activities that help them progress toward the next learning level; and using a variety of instructional strategies, adapted equipment, and learning environments to meet their diverse needs.

This chapter addresses approaches to planning and implementing quality aquatic activities that meet the needs of the widest array of learners possible. You will learn to look at your aquatic curriculum and swim lessons through the lens of universal design and to provide instruction and learning activities that break down barriers to learning. A flexible approach to meeting the challenges, interests, and needs of the variety of people who want to learn to swim helps aquatics instructors reach more people in the quest to make everyone safe and successful in the water. Consider incorporating these concepts into your own activities, and keep them in mind as you view the activities in part II of this book.

This chapter begins with a description of universal design in terms of pool access and learning. Next, the chapter addresses differentiation of instruction and then delves into tips for meeting the more intense needs of learners such as those who are afraid of the water and those with profound physical and cognitive impairments.

Universal Design

The Center for Universal Design defines universal design as products and environments that all people can use without the need for adaptation or specialized design; this led to its coining the term *universal usability* (1997). Several universal design principles provide a framework for exploring how to make aquatic centers and pools usable to all. Facility use should be equitable, flexible, easy, and intuitive.

Ron Mace, the originator of the universal design concept, suggested that universal design is not about modifying spaces and products to conform with the Americans with Disabilities Act, but rather is the incorporation of these principles from the beginning of the design process (Mace, 1998). Universally designed pools are available to everyone. The concept of universal design for facilities and products is the genesis for the concept of *universal design for learning* that will be introduced later in this chapter.

Universal Design for Pool Access

Universal design for aquatic activities begins with pool access. Because of the diversity of patrons, pools should have multiple options available; examples include ramps, zero-depth entries, and lifts.

A zero-depth entry is like entering the water at the beach—that is, people can walk, scoot, or wheel themselves into the pool without the need for a lift, stairs, or a ladder. The pool deck transitions gradually into the pool bottom without a lip or barrier to obstruct entering or exiting. In addition to meeting the concept of universal design, a zero-depth entry (also called a wet ramp or in-pool ramp) is one of two methods mandated in the Americans with Disabilities Act

A pool that has universal design will provide pool fun and activity to everyone.

as a "primary means" of access to swimming pools. (ADA guidelines state that the slope must be no greater than 1 inch [2.5 cm] of rise and 12 inches [30.5] of length.) A zero-depth entry must be available in the absence of a pool lift. Unfortunately, not many pools are designed this way.

A pool lift is a mechanical device with a plastic chair that can be powered by a battery or water; it is used to assist a person into and out of the pool. This primary means of access must be available in the absence of a zero-depth entry.

Other means of entry and exit are considered "secondary means of access" by the Americans with Disabilities Act. They include ADA-compliant stairs, transfer tiers, and transfer walls. More information about these means of access can be found in *Adapted Aquatics Programming: A Professional Guide* (Lepore, Gayle, & Stevens, 1997).

Universal Design for Learning

Borrowing from the field of architectural design, the education field coined the term *universal design for learning* to denote ways teachers can reach a wider audience of learners. The concept behind universal design for learning is that every learner should be considered in the curriculum-planning process. This approach to pedagogy guides teachers in designing instructional experiences that give all learners equal opportunities to learn, demonstrate what they have learned, and participate in learning activities to practice what they have learned. Universal design for learning is about providing a variety of ways to learn instead of using a "one size fits all" approach.

Universal design for learning has the potential to remove barriers to participation in aquatic activities by encouraging instructors to consider alternative teaching methods and, as a result, aquatic curricula. It provides greater access to programs for students with a variety of learning, physical, emotional, and social characteristics. Following the principles of universal design for learning, aquatics instructors design curricula, lessons, and activities to accommodate a wide range of learners, although modifications and adaptations would be only for those learners with the most intense needs (differences). Instructors who consider students with a variety of ability levels during the planning of games and activities often discover that the changes to traditional activities help all learners.

Consider a class of 10 students in which three students have a need to know what is going to happen before the lesson to help them with their behavior and focus. The instructor can write the schedule and topics of the day on a whiteboard in the pool area for everyone to see. All students benefit from this, not only the students with learning disabilities. Coach DJ did things like this in the opening scenario. This is an example of universal design for learning because it provides an accommodation for a small number of students as part of the regular instruction; meanwhile, all students benefit.

Consider the following when planning for universally designed aquatic activities:

- Not all learners are successful in the same way in the same activities.
- Students have an assortment of strengths, needs, and interests as well as a variety of aquatic experiences.

Rose and Meyer (2002) suggested that universally designed lessons and activities should provide multiple, flexible methods of presenting information, means of expression, and options for engagement.

Using the concept of universal design requires eliminating barriers to participation before presenting a lesson or activity, not modifying it after it is designed. Consider an activity that focuses on using a kickboard to practice kicking. If one of the students has no arms, the instructor can change the focus from how to use a kickboard to how to practice the kick. In addition to using a kickboard, students can use a pool noodle under the chest, a barbell float, or no flotation device at all. Considering all the learners in a class for each part of the lesson helps instructors design physical, social, and learning environments that meet all students' needs (McGuire, Scott, & Shaw, 2006). Before implementing the universal design for learning approach to aquatic instruction, the instructor must answer these three questions (Lieberman, Lytle, & Clarcq, 2008, p. 34):

- What is the functional ability of each learner?
- What are the general class objectives and the individual objectives of the learners?
- What parts of the activity or lesson can be modified?

Aquatics instructors should embrace the fundamental principles of universal design for learning to ensure that all students benefit from physical activity (Columna & Lieberman, 2011), especially in swimming and aquatic units.

Differentiation of Instruction

One practice that helps teachers incorporate universal design for learning into their teaching is called differentiation of instruction. Rather than being simply a set of instructional strategies, differentiation of instruction is about giving students multiple options for taking in information, understanding ideas, and showing what they have learned (Tomlinson, 2001). This process requires that teachers recognize the diverse abilities within their groups of students and maximize all students' growth by meeting them, individually, where they are in the learning process (Hall, Strangman, & Meyer, 2003). Differentiation of aquatic instruction involves addressing elements such as the environment, the curriculum, skill assessments, class management, and instruction.

Differentiation is not about the content taught, but about how instructors deliver it using multiple cues, formats, explanations, assessments, equipment, environments, and strategies (Tomlinson, 1999b). "Differentiating instruction focuses on taking the content, learning activities, outcomes, and environment and providing specific adaptations to meet the needs of varying ability learners in your swim class" (Ellis, Lieberman, & LeRoux, 2009; p. 19). This allows aquatics instructors to create lesson plans for the entire class while modifying the delivery and how students practice and demonstrate what they have learned (assessment).

The following examples, modified from Tomlinson (2001), show several ways in which to differentiate learning:

- Create and deliver instructions carefully. Think through the instructions; anticipate problems students might have and prepare modifications for these.
- Provide clear expectations and time lines.
- Assign groups and partners rather than have students select their own.
- Give clear directions about how to move to an assigned group (i.e., where it meets).
- Designate a home base for students to go back to for instructions and at the beginning and end of the lesson.
- Have a signal for when to listen and when to keep the noise down.
- Request that students who find the pool area too noisy bring earplugs.
- State clearly when you want the students to finish with a task and what they should do and where they should go when finished.
- Define what on-task behavior looks like and promote it by giving cues and incentives.

Students With Intense Needs

By universally designing curricula, lessons, activities, and practice sessions, instructors can expect to reach approximately 80 percent of their students. On occasions, they will meet students who are extremely fearful or have intense disability needs. These students require greater intervention, including smaller instructor-to-student (or assistant-to-student) ratios, additional analyses of skills, more carefully planned or modified progressions, equipment adaptations, and possibly auxiliary aids and services.

Instructor-to-Student Ratios

During typical swim lessons, depending on the students' ages and skill levels, most groups have between a 1:4 and a 1:12 instructor-to-student ratio. When a student is not safe or successful in a typical swim lesson environment, even if the lessons have been universally designed and differentiated, more intense supervision is needed. This can be accomplished by decreasing the number of students in a group to give the one student more attention and lessen distractions; as a result, many students can then achieve a higher level of learning. Bringing in an instructional assistant to provide more physical and instructional support will also improve the instructor-to-student ratio. For some students a group is not the best environment in which to learn; these students may require one-on-one instruction. Bringing in someone with expertise in adapted aquatics (i.e., an instructor with experience and credentials in teaching those with disabilities) might be necessary for some students.

Task Analysis of Skills

Students with learning and physical needs might need skills to be broken down into smaller segments (task analysis of skills), as can be done using the modified Texas Woman's University aquatic assessment referenced in this book. Consider skill 3.11 in level 3 (glide on back and recover to feet with instructor support). This skill could be divided into the following parts:

- The student holds the wall with two hands while facing the wall.
- The student crouches down to shoulder level in the water while holding the wall.
- The student places the soles of both feet approximately 18 inches (45.7 cm) below where their hands are on the wall.
- The student extends the neck backward so the back of the head is in the water.
- The student curls up in a ball, bending the knees and elbows, with the back of the head still in the water.
- The student releases the wall with both hands, extends the knees, and pushes off backward with the back of the head still in the water.
- The student glides in a horizontal position for at least 5 feet (1.5 m) with the hands tight at the sides in a streamlined position.

Breaking a skill into very small parts helps students with behavioral or cognitive limitations concentrate on one thing at a time.

Modified Progressions

A progression is a pathway of learning that leads the student to a goal. For example, kicking is typically taught beginning in a stationary position holding the pool gutter or the side of the pool. (Some pools are flush with the deck and do not have gutters.) Then students progress to holding the instructor's shoulders, and then to a kickboard or pool noodle pulled by the instructor. They then work independently with a kickboard and, finally, practice kicking as part of a swim stroke.

With students who have more intense physical, behavioral, or learning challenges, instructors may need to try different approaches. The Halliwick concept, devised by James McMillan, is a holistic approach to teaching swimming that combines hydrodynamic principles, hydrostatics, and kinesiology in a mind–body approach that focuses on getting comfortable and being "water happy" (Halliwick Association of Swimming Therapy, 2002). The basis of the concept is a 10-point program; students must master each point to be considered "water happy." The 10 points are as follows:

1. *Mental adjustment*—responding to various environments, situations, and tasks in a flexible and relaxed manner. Physical and mental adjustments and breath control are addressed in this point.

2. *Disengagement*—being independent when moving in the water.

3. *Transversal rotational control*—gaining the body control needed to maintain a balanced position when moving from a horizontal to a vertical and back to a horizontal position in the water.

4. *Sagittal rotational control*—gaining the body control needed to recover from falling to the right or left in the water.

5. *Longitudinal rotational control*—gaining the body control needed to maintain a balanced position when turning around the long axis of the body (i.e., spinning like a top).

6. *Combined rotation control*—being able to keep control over your body when it begins to roll to the right and left (such as rolling over in bed) and forwards and backwards (such as doing a forward or backward somersault). Controlling your body so it does not spin in any direction is important to maintaining postural control to move on to higher level skills in swim stroke instruction.

7. *Upthrust*—trusting that the water will support you.

8. *Balance in stillness*—being relaxed while lying still in the water.

9. *Turbulent gliding*—controlling the body while being pulled along by an instructor drafting the swimmer. Drafting is when a swimmer is on her back or front with an instructor a few inches from the swimmers head, and the instructor runs backward, creating a "draft" that moves the swimmer toward the instructor without physical contact.

10. *Simple progression and basic swim stroke*—putting what you learned through this progressive method to use in performing swim strokes.

The Halliwick concept has been instrumental in helping those who are afraid of the water and those with physical and learning disabilities accept water as a friend. Moving along the 10-point progression develops a cornerstone for progressing to more mainstream aquatic skills and swim strokes. For additional information, visit http://halliwick.org.

Modified progressions can help students with special needs become comfortable in the water.

Equipment Adaptations

When universally designing learning experiences and instructional activities, instructors need to provide equipment in a wide variety of shapes, sizes, weights, colors, lengths, widths, and textures to differentiate instruction. Meeting the needs of a variety of students forces instructors to think outside the box in terms of equipment selection and usage. For students with more intense physical and learning needs, the instructor must search for equipment that would not typically be available in a general recreational or instructional aquatic program. Equipment adaptations can be devised and created by instructors, students, or students' families, or purchased from a variety of vendors.

To determine the type of equipment that would help a student, instructors should ask themselves what the purpose of the equipment is. Following are some choices:

- Fun and motivation
- Flotation
- Support
- Fitness and exercise
- Propulsion
- Safety
- Entry or exit from the pool

More information on equipment modification is available in *Adapted Aquatics Programming: A Professional Guide* (Lepore, Gayle, & Stevens, 2007).

Supplementary Aids and Services

If smaller instructor-to-student ratios, breaking skills into smaller segments, modified progressions, differentiated instruction, and modified equipment or supplies are not working, it may be time to add supplementary aids and services to aquatic instruction. This mandate comes out of the Individuals with Disabilities Education Act (IDEA), a U.S. education law that guarantees special education services for children with disabilities. IDEA requires "services or other supports that provide students with disabilities accommodations or modifications that can directly support a student to meet the goals and objectives of the regular education curriculum and be educated with their peers to the maximum extent possible" (Sec. 650 [1] [11] [B]). Following are examples of supplementary aids and services that might be helpful in the aquatic setting:

- Specialized equipment specific to a student
- An instructor with expertise in adapted aquatics
- Different pacing of instruction
- Environmental adaptations such as quiet locations or distraction-free zones
- Large-print or braille formats
- Lesson outlines provided in advance
- Social skills support
- Specialized training for instructional personnel

The level of involvement of supplementary aids and services is dictated by whether the aquatic program is a school-based program (regulated by IDEA) or a community-based program (regulated by ADA).

Summary

This chapter explored a variety of strategies for helping everyone make progress in aquatic activities, including universally designed facilities and lessons; differentiated instruction; modifications to tasks, progressions, and equipment; and supplemental support. Instructors should begin their interactions with students by assessing them to determine their levels of performance so they can determine how best to help them build their skills.

This chapter concluded with additional resources to help instructors provide successful aquatic experiences to all students.

Resources

Books

American Red Cross. (2009). *Swimming and water safety.* Yardley, PA: Stay Well.

Barth, K., & Dietze, J. (2004). *Learning swimming.* Aachen, Germany: Meyer & Meyer Verlag.

Grosse, S. (2007). *Water learning.* Champaign, IL: Human Kinetics.

Lees, T. (2007). *Water fun.* Champaign, IL: Human Kinetics.

Myers, M. (2011). *The big book of swimming pool games.* Distributed by Amazon Digital Services.

Noble, J., & Cregeen, A. (2004). *Swimming—games and activities.* London: A & C Black.

Noble, J., & Cregeen, A. (2009). *Swimming—games and activities: For parents and teachers.* London: A & C Black.

Websites

Basic Adapted Aquatic Activities and Games. This manual is for teachers of students with disabilities. It complements the aquatics sections of Project INSPIRE, Texas Woman's University's program for people with special needs and TWU's aquatic skills assessment.

www.twu.edu/downloads/inspire/Aquatics_Manual_Intro_1.pdf

eHow. A variety of games appropriate for aquatic environments.

www.ehow.com/way_5312518_games-play-during-swim-lessons.html

LIVESTRONG. This website has a variety of health tips such as good food choices, lifestyle plans, and a calorie tracker. It also gives in-depth descriptions of great pool games to play with kids in class.

www.livestrong.com/article/144566-childrens-pool-games

PELinks4U. This website geared toward secondary education has a variety of pool activities as well as comments from teachers about each. It also has a section called Sun Safety 101.

www.pelinks4u.org/archives/secondary/060104.htm

swimmingpool.com. This website has everything you need to throw a pool party: ideas for a theme, drinks, food, decorations, games, and invitations.

www.swimmingpool.com/entertaining/pool-games

Ultimate Camp Resource. A list of games that can be played in the water.

www.ultimatecampresource.com/site/camp-activities/water-games.page-1.html

uSwim. A website geared to teaching infants, toddlers, and children to swim.

www.uswim.com

Assessment: The Foundation for Swimming Instruction

Allie is a five-year-old who has taken aquatic orientation classes since she was six months old. She can can tread water for short bouts; perform the initial phase of many aquatic skills such as bobbing, the front crawl, the back glide, and the flutter kick; and has adequate pool entry and exit skills. She is registered for the kindergarten after-school swim class and says she is excited to learn to dive, sit on the bottom of the shallow end for a tea party, and swim the butterfly.

Toby is a five-year-old who has not had access to swim classes and is comfortable only holding his parents' hands and wading waist deep into the pool. He is hesitant to go down the ladder independently and does not like to get water on his face and in his ears. He is signed up for the same kindergarten after-school swim class as Allie. Toby hopes the instructor lets him use some arm swimmies to hold him up. He is looking forward to learning how to doggie paddle the width of the pool.

It is apparent that these two students will need to be instructed at different levels and to progress to different skills. Yet swim instructors commonly begin their lessons the same way for everyone. Without performing assessments, the instructor might not tailor the instruction and the content appropriately, and Toby may be too scared to participate while Allie might be too bored to want to continue. Assessment is needed to determine the appropriate skill progression for each of these young learners.

What Is Assessment?

Assessment is the process of gathering information to determine the level of performance of a person in a particular environment (i.e., his strengths and his needs). It is also the process of monitoring a person's progress in performing a particular skill. In an aquatic environment, this involves identifying the aquatic abilities of learners at the initial stage and monitoring their progress throughout the program.

This chapter describes ways to assess the skills of students of varying ability levels using the modified Texas Woman's University (TWU) aquatic assessment. This assessment served as a framework for the development of the activities in the remainder of the book.

To provide successful aquatic experiences, instructors need to conduct comprehensive initial assessments so they can document students' learning. Teachers, parents, and aquatics instructors can use assessment results for many purposes, including determining learners' strengths and the areas in which they require improvement.

In aquatic environments, the techniques (form and style) of swimming strokes are typically assessed (Grosse, 2005). However, some physical education instructors, recreation specialists, and parents may not have a background in aquatics or know how to assess aquatic abilities. This chapter can help. The modified version of the TWU aquatic assessment is used in this book to identify the aquatic skills and activities that are important to assess. The assessment process is addressed in the next section of this chapter, which also includes an explanation of how to use the assessment with the activities outlined in the rest of the book. The activities, along with the modified TWU aquatic assessment, will help instructors and parents teach their students and children appropriate aquatic skills.

Before starting instruction in aquatic activities, instructors need to conduct assessments to identify what the student knows about swimming. However, before starting your assessment, you need to identify the assessment instrument you will use and the equipment you will need. You also need to gather information about the student while developing a rapport with him or her. The TWU aquatic assessment is one of several that can be used in aquatics; it is both the focus of this chapter and the impetus for the creation of this book.

The Modified TWU Aquatic Assessment

The TWU aquatic assessment, designed by Dr. Carol Huettig in 1998, is a curriculum-based assessment instrument that addresses the following:

- Water adjustment skills
- Flotation skills
- Basic propulsion and breathing skills
- Swimm stroke skills
- Entry and exit skills

Skills in each of these five categories progress in a hierarchical fashion (from simple to complex) to the acquisition of the next skill (Columna, 2011).

This assessment instrument is divided into six levels. Level 1 is the simplest, and level 6 is the most advanced. We propose using the modified TWU assessment instrument for three reasons: (1) it has been used successfully by many aquatics professionals, (2) it is very easy to use, and (3) it is free. Keep in mind that, as a parent or instructor, you should not consider yourself an expert on assessment after reading this book; that would require additional training. The goal of this book is to help you teach aquatic activities to your child or student. We are not trying to replace professional aquatics instructors or programs. We also recommend that you perform your assessments in a community pool with a lifeguard on duty.

Levels of the Assessment

This section provides brief descriptions of each level of the modified TWU assessment. It is followed by a discussion of how to match the assessment to the activities in part II.

Level 1

Aquatic environments can be overwhelming for young children or those with intellectual or learning disabilities. Level 1 provides a gentle introduction to the water to create a positive, successful experience for beginning swimmers. For those with no previous experience in the water, level 1 introduces 24 basic aquatic skills to help the student acclimate to the aquatic environment. This level starts with activities that involve playing with toys on the pool deck with no interaction with the water. Eventually, the activities include walking, jumping, and even running in the water. Once students are comfortable in the water, they are shown how to blow bubbles and pick up objects from underwater.

Level 2

Once students have mastered the activities in level 1, they proceed to level 2. Those who can already perform the skills required for level 1 can begin instruction at level 2. As in level 1, students in level 2 perform 24 swimming skills, although in this level they include bobbing, floating, kicking, and jumping. For many beginner swimmers, the most difficult skills are floating faceup or facedown. Floating faceup is the most challenging skill in this level.

Level 3

Level 3 is the typical entry level for most students who sign up for swim lessons; those with previous recreational experiences with their families tend to start

at level 3. This level includes a review of some skills introduced in level 2, such as bobbing, but then takes these skills to a higher level. Additional skills presented at this level include rhythmic breathing and gliding. These two skills are essential for progressing to the more advanced swimming skills, such as the front crawl. Level 3 addresses 23 swimming skills, including combining breathing and gliding while performing the front crawl, and progresses to the integration of the flutter kick.

The most difficult skills at this level are jumping into deep water, treading water, and full body submersion. These skills are prerequisites for the safety skills and the more advanced skills that are introduced at the remaining levels.

Students progress into the deep end in level 3.

Level 4

Level 4 includes 17 skills. Similar to levels 2 and 3, students at level 4 perform more advanced versions of some of the skills they were introduced to earlier. Skills at this level include the front crawl, elementary backstroke, and breaststroke. The primary difference between levels 3 and 4 is that students are required to perform skills for longer periods of time and for longer distances in level 4. In addition, students combine key skills such as breathing and kicking.

Level 5 and Level 6

Once students reach levels 5 and 6, they can participate in competitive sports and take part in more advanced aquatic activities. All of the skills students need to successfully and safely participate in aquatic environments are tested at these two levels. Skills such as the front crawl, back crawl, breaststroke, sidestroke, and butterfly are the same skills swimmers need to compete on teams.

Conducting the Assessment

Before starting the assessment, laminate the assessment form so that it does not get wet. Use a permanent, fine-point marker to make your annotations on the form. You can then scan the form and save it on a computer or transfer the assessment by to any other form of record keeping.

Before assessing students, develop a rapport with them. You can also collect information from their parents or guardians, either by interview (phone or in person) or by sending a survey or questionnaire to the home. Inquire about the student's ability level, preferred activities, family composition, behavioral tendencies, and communication preferences. Collecting this information from the family can save time during assessment and instruction (Columna, 2011). Students themselves can be a great source of information as well, although swimmers with severe disabilities or speech impairments may ned additional assistance to express their desires. Columna (2011) provides a questionnaire to use to obtain information about students (see figure 2.1).

Once you are familiar with the criteria for the assessment and have developed a sense of trust with the student, you are ready to start conducting the assessment. Because of varying levels of ability, not all assessment items are suited for all students. You may need to modify the assessment to meet the needs of certain students. As mentioned previously, one of the main reasons to assess students is to determine their present level of performance (what they can do) in a variety of skills. Feel free to modify the way you perform the assessment, such as giving directions more than once, doing additional demonstrations, providing assistance for initial trials of a skill, letting the student take a break, or skipping a skill that the student is frightened to perform.

Teachers assessing a large number of students will benefit from the help of paraeducators (assistants), especially if some students have disabilities that affect their performance in the pool. Teachers should identify students who will need assistance performing an activity and when that assistance will be needed. Some students might need assistance for some of the assessment activities, but not for all of them.

Parents and instructors who are assessing students on their own might find technology handy. The instructor can ask a parent to be a helper during the assessment process and record a video of the assessment so the instructor can later review the video with the assessment checklist. Using a video to assess allows you to stay focused on working with the student, which can be helpful

General Information

Aquatics

True = T
False = F
Not sure = N

_____ My child is comfortable in/loves the water.

_____ My child is afraid of the water.

_____ My child does not know how to swim and does not display a respectful understanding of the water.

_____ My child is able to put his or her face in the water.

_____ My child is not able to put his or her face in the water.

_____ My child is able to enter the water independently.

_____ My child is able to swim in shallow water.

_____ My child is able to swim in deep water.

Expressive Communication

Primary language: _____ English _____ Spanish _____ Other: _____
True = T
False = F
Not sure = N

_____ The swimmer has clear and understandable speech.

_____ The swimmer talks in short sentences.

_____ The swimmer talks in short phrases or uses single words.

_____ The swimmer has little verbal speech but uses effective gestures.

_____ The swimmer has little or no functional speech.

_____ The swimmer uses a communication board with cards and pictures.

_____ The swimmer uses sign language. If so, what signs does he or she use?

Receptive Communication

True = T
False = F
Not sure = N

_____ The swimmer is able to follow complex directions (three or four steps).

_____ The swimmer is able to follow simple verbal directions.

_____ The swimmer understands short phrases or uses single words.

_____ The swimmer understands effective gestures.

_____ The swimmer does not appear to understand speech.

(continued)

Figure 2.1 Example of parent questionnaire. Please feel free to modify this questionnaire to suit your needs.

_____ The swimmer understands communication with a board or pictures.

_____ The swimmer understands sign language. If so, what signs does he or she understand?

_____

Behavior

True = T
False = F
Not sure = N

_____ The swimmer is generally cooperative and follows adult directions.

_____ The swimmer requires minimal supervision to remain on task.

_____ The swimmer needs constant supervision to stay on task.

_____ The swimmer is easily distracted and has difficulty staying on task.

_____ The swimmer may refuse to follow directions.

_____ The swimmer may have a temper tantrum.*

_____ The swimmer may become verbally or physically aggressive.*

*What type of incident(s) typically triggers the behavior?

_____

_____

Special Equipment

True = T
False = F
Not sure = N

My child uses the following:

_____ Motorized or manual wheelchair

_____ Walker or crutches. Please note type: _____

_____ Prosthesis. Please note location: _____

_____ Braces. Please note location: _____

_____ Hearing aid

_____ Earplugs

_____ Protective helmet

_____ Contact lenses or glasses

_____ Cochlear implant

_____ White cane (for swimmers who are blind or visually impaired)

From M. Lepore, L. Columna, and L. Friedlander Litzner, 2015, _Assessments and activities for teaching swimming_ (Champaign, IL: Human Kinetics). From L. Columna, 2011, "Assessing aquatics." In _Assessment for everyone._ Adapted with permission from the Society of Health and Physical Educators (SHAPE America), 1900 Association Drive, Reston, VA 20191, www.shapeamerica.org.

Figure 2.1 _(continued)_

when working with people who are afraid of being in the water, those with behavioral problems, and those with severe disabilities.

Using the Modified TWU Aquatic Assessment

This section explains how to use the Modified TWU Aquatic Assessment at level 1 to demonstrate the process (see figure 2.2). At the top of each level of the modified TWU aquatic assessment is general information: the name and age of the student, the date, and the instructor's name. The rest provides skill descriptions and provides a way to take notes.

The first column identifies the page number where the skill is to be found. The second column lists the skill number (e.g., 1.1, 1.2, 1.3). The third column provides a description of the skill the student is to perform or master. In either the fourth or fifth column, instructors check yes or no to indicate whether the student was able to perform the skill. The last column provides space to add any comments to support the assessment findings. For example, if, when playing with toys on the pool deck (skill 1.1), a child demonstrates a preference for or disinterest in a particular toy, this information can be included in the comments section. Not all skills will need additional comments. Use your personal judgment to decide what information will help you recall the student's performance.

If you are teaching a student with no aquatic experience, depending on the age of the student, start with level 1 (especially with young children with or

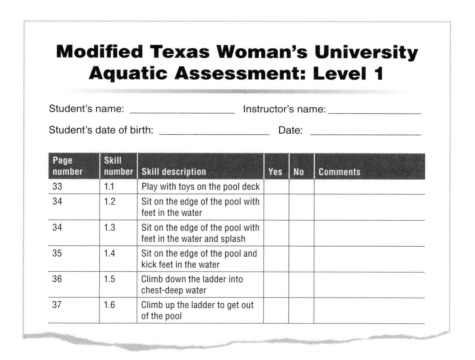

Modified Texas Woman's University Aquatic Assessment: Level 1

Student's name: _____   Instructor's name: _____

Student's date of birth: _____   Date: _____

Page number	Skill number	Skill description	Yes	No	Comments
33	1.1	Play with toys on the pool deck			
34	1.2	Sit on the edge of the pool with feet in the water			
34	1.3	Sit on the edge of the pool with feet in the water and splash			
35	1.4	Sit on the edge of the pool and kick feet in the water			
36	1.5	Climb down the ladder into chest-deep water			
37	1.6	Climb up the ladder to get out of the pool			

Figure 2.2   Level 1 assessment. The full version of this assessment can be found at the start of level 1.

without disabilities). For older students or those with previous aquatic experience, you may decide to start by assessing the most advanced skills in level 1 or skills in level 2. The information provided by the family on the family survey can help you choose. Never put students into deep water until you have assessed their ability to tread water and bob in chin-deep water.

Let's consider the two young children described in the opening scenarios of this chapter (Allie and Toby). From the family survey and a conversation with Allie's parents, you learn that Allie has played in a pool every summer since age 2, and she loves the water. Therefore, there is no need to start on the first skill (1.1), which has students playing with toys on the pool deck. Your assessment might involve asking Allie to enter the water and perform the highest skill on the level 1 assessment (picking up a ring from the bottom of the pool in the shallow end). Make sure you supervise her carefully. If Allie can perform this task, you can move on to level 2.

Toby's parents, meanwhile, have indicated that he has never taken formal swimming lessons and has little to no exposure to an aquatic environment. Toby should therefore start at level 1, skill 1.1, playing with toys on the pool deck.

This assessment process holds true for all of the levels in this book. You can move forward or backward in the levels using your personal judgment (with safety in mind) to determine the level at which a student should start. If you are still not sure of the level, you can ask a professional aquatics instructor or start at a lower level and proceed from there. In Toby's case, you could start assessing him at skill 1.1 and see how many level 1 skills he can perform.

Let's look at one more example. Let's say you are assessing a boy who is comfortable moving in the water, so you skip to either skill 1.16 (hop three times on the preferred foot independently) to determine balance, or to skill 1.21 (place the face in the water without holding on to anything). If the boy performs these skills, you may be able to move him to level 2. If he is hesitant to place his face in the water without holding on to anything, move back in level 1 to skill 1.17 (pretend to wash the face with water). If the boy can perform this skill, then you move to skill 1.18 (blow a ping-pong ball on the water surface). Generally speaking, if the student can perform the skill, you can move deeper into the assessment.

In some parts of the assessment the next skill is unrelated to the skill just assessed. For example, skill 1.16 (hop) and skill 1.17 (washing or wetting the face) are not progressions of the same skill. If a girl cannot perform skill 1.16, it does not mean that she cannot perform skill 1.17. She may not be able to perform skill 1.16 because she has motor skill difficulties, is an amputee, or has paralysis, but she may still be able to wet her face. If this occurs during your assessment, don't stop. Be aware that some students have splinter skills (i.e., can perform a skill at one level but not another). If the skill in the level you are using is not based on the next skill (e.g., blowing bubbles is not a prerequisite to kicking), you might need to reexamine the assessment to make sure it is appropriate.

After the Assessment

Once you have obtained as much information as you can from the modified TWU aquatic assessment and from the interviews with the student and, if applicable, the family, you are ready to determine the level the student should be working on (i.e., the level at which you will begin teaching). At this point, write a paragraph about the student's skill level, list his strengths and needs (weaknesses), and write a few goals for him to achieve based on what he has not completed at that level. If you are an instructor, discuss your placement decision with the family and the student, if appropriate, and come to an agreement on what you will teach.

For Allie, the instructor wrote the following about her present level of performance and her strengths and needs:

> Allie is a five-year-old entering the WCU swim program with all skills complete in level 1 and 50 percent of the skills accomplished in level 2. She is comfortable in the water, excited to learn new skills, and practices skills when given motivation to stay on task longer than two minutes. Allie loves submerging to the bottom of the pool in 3 feet (1 m) of water and grasping a ring, and she is able to complete 12 of the 24 skills in level 2.

Strengths
- Independent entry and exit including using the pool ladder and sitting on the side of the pool and sliding in

Assess the level of comfort of a child in shallow water before moving on to more difficult skills in the deep end of the pool.

- Independent locomotor skills in 3-foot (1 m) depth
- Submersion in 3-foot (1 m) depth
- Floating facedown and faceup with assistance

Needs
- Floating facedown and faceup independently
- Jumping in from the side
- Exiting the pool without the use of the ladder

During the next eight weeks of swim lessons, Allie will do the following:

- Improve her pool exit on the side of the pool until she can do it independently at least one out of five tries by the end of the eight-week session
- Improve floating faceup and facedown independently and perform both for at least five seconds by the end of the eight-week session
- Improve her water entry by jumping into chest-deep water independently at least once in the eight-week session

For Toby, the instructor wrote the following:

Toby is a five-year-old boy who is entering the WCU swim program as a novice without any prior swim instruction. He was able to complete 13 of the 24 level 1 skills; most of the skills require instructor assistance. He is not able to submerge his face or perform any of the locomotor skills independently. Toby was cautious during the assessment. His attitude suggests that he is fearful but wants to learn to swim.

Strengths

- Independent entry and exit using the ladder
- Performance of locomotor skills with instructor assistance or using the pool wall or gutter
- Positive attitude

Needs

- Being comfortable with water on his face
- Submerging underwater
- Being independent moving about the pool

During the next eight weeks of swim lessons, Toby will make progress toward the following:

- Submerging his full body underwater for three seconds by the end of the eight-week session
- Performing independent motor skills in the shallow end of the pool as shown by running the width of the pool and hopping three times in 3-foot (1 m) depth by the end of the eight-week session

Once you identify the skills and the level at which you need to work with students, you need to plan the activities to which you will expose them to improve their aquatic skills. Now it is time to teach your students the skills they need to improve or develop.

Summary

This chapter presented the keys to implementing the assessments and activities in this book. Assessment is important to the planning of developmentally appropriate activities for the student or students with whom you are working. By gathering information, getting to know the student, selecting the appropriate level at which to begin your assessment, observing carefully during the assessment, and setting goals for the student, you will be on your way to providing enjoyable and productive aquatic activities.

PART II

Aquatic Activities for Everyone

Part II provides fun and exciting activities that motivate students to demonstrate their skills so you can assess and help them to improve their swim skills. The 206 developmentally appropriate aquatic activities presented in levels 1 through 6 parallel the six levels of swimming designated by the modified Texas Woman's University (TWU) aquatic assessment.

The activities in part II are organized by skills. Each skill includes a description and verbal cues and differentiation ideas (i.e., ways to modify the activities). Each activity includes a list of the equipment needed, an explanation of any preparation needed, a description of where the students and instructor are situated (formation), and descriptions of what the instructor and students do during the activity.

Getting Started With Water Fun

Modified Texas Woman's University Aquatic Assessment: Level 1

Student's name: _____ Instructor's name: _____

Student's date of birth: _____ Date: _____

Page number	Skill number	Skill description	Yes	No	Comments
33	1.1	Play with toys on the pool deck			
34	1.2	Sit on the edge of the pool with feet in the water			
34	1.3	Sit on the edge of the pool with feet in the water and splash			
35	1.4	Sit on the edge of the pool and kick feet in the water			
36	1.5	Climb down the ladder into chest-deep water			
37	1.6	Climb up the ladder to get out of the pool			
38	1.7	Walk at least 12 yards holding the pool gutter or edge			
39	1.8	Walk in chest-deep water at least 12 yards holding the instructor's hand			
39	1.9	Walk across the pool independently			
40	1.10	Run across the pool independently			
42	1.11	Turn in a circle in chest-deep water			
43	1.12	Jump three times holding the instructor's hand			
44	1.13	Jump three times independently			
44	1.14	Jump continuously in chest-deep water for at least 12 yards independently			
45	1.15	Hop three times on the preferred foot, holding the instructor's hand			
45	1.16	Hop three times on the preferred foot independently			
46	1.17	Pretend to wash the face with water			

Page number	Skill number	Skill description	Yes	No	Comments
47	1.18	Blow a ping-pong ball on the water surface			
48	1.19	Blow bubbles on the water surface			
48	1.20	Place the face in the water while holding the gutter or pool edge			
49	1.21	Place the face in the water without holding on to anything			
50	1.22	Blow bubbles, breathe, and blow bubbles			
50	1.23	Blow bubbles, breathe, and blow bubbles three times in a row			
51	1.24	Pick up a ring (or other object) from the bottom of the pool			

General comments:

Modified from Texas Woman's University Aquatic Assessment.

From M. Lepore, L. Columna, and L. Friedlander Litzner, 2015, *Assessments and activities for teaching swimming* (Champaign, IL: Human Kinetics).

Now that you understand some of the benefits of aquatics, have learned strategies to present aquatic skills, and understand the importance of assessment, part II brings you to the meat of the book—descriptions of exciting aquatic activities that correspond with the assessment in chapter 2. To reiterate, assessments are crucial for all students both to establish learning goals and to determine where to begin teaching. When you find that a student has not achieved a certain task, go to the activity that is suggested for that assessment level, explain and demonstrate the skill, and then present the activity to help the student develop and practice that skill.

As previously mentioned, aquatic environments can be overwhelming to some young children and some people with disabilities. A gentle introduction to the water can motivate these students and promote a positive experience. Level 1 provides 24 swim skills to introduce students to aquatics and its wonders.

Once you have conducted a preassessment and have identified the student's strengths and areas that need improvement, the fun begins. You don't need to do all the activities in this chapter; rather, use those that meet the interests, developmental level, age, and swimming ability of the student. For example, not all reluctant students should play with toys on the pool deck (skill 1.1) because not all will be very young children or be interested in toys (or be children at all). Use your judgment to decide where to start. As much as possible, discuss with students what they believe they can and cannot do and which activities seem fun to them.

Lastly, the activities in this level represent general ideas for making the aquatic experience fun. Feel free to modify any of them and to develop some of your own.

Modifying Activities for Use With Older Students

If you are teaching older beginning students, your games and equipment need to be age appropriate. For example, you can replace floating toys with more adult-appropriate props such as kickboards and nursery rhymes with top 40 music. Most adults are more motivated by social praise than by toys and equipment.

Pool and Water Orientation

Nonswimmers and swimmers who have had frightening aquatic experiences may be hesitant to get into the water during the first few swim sessions. Introducing them to "wet play" on the pool deck with toys or other interesting water play objects (appropriate to their age) can help these students transition gradually from being dry to being wet. They can play while sitting on the edge of the pool and gradually be encouraged to climb up and down the ladder.

Cues for Playing With Toys on the Pool Deck

- Put these toys in the water bucket.
- Wash your hands in the bucket.
- Take your time and relax with the toys.
- Show your family how you can paint my hands with the water brush.

Cues for Using the Ladder

- Hold the railings when going up and down the ladder.
- Take one step at a time.

Differentiation for Playing With Toys in the Pool Deck

- Have a family member or assistant provide support to those with balance issues or those who have difficulty sitting still.
- For students with visual impairments, a rope with tape on top of it provides a tactile reference point. This will allow the swimmer to orient and have access to the pool deck, pool walls, and toys.
- For activities that require holding hands, if additional support is needed, hold the forearms or trunk of the student (for those who cannot use or do not have hands).
- Demonstrate, simplify, and repeat the instructions.

Differentiation for Using the Ladder

- Instead of a wall ladder, students can use a removable, gradual staircase (if available).
- Support the student by the trunk or back.
- Students who cannot use the ladder can use a pool lift.

Visiting With Water Creatures

Skill 1.1—Play With Toys on the Pool Deck

Equipment
Pool toys, pool noodles

Preparation
Place a variety of interesting, age-appropriate items such as plastic animals, waterproof sea creatures, rubber ducks or frogs, pool noodles, and kickboards on the pool deck.

Formation
The student is sitting on the pool deck facing the instructor in a safe, low-traffic area that is close to a pool entry point.

Instructor Directions
Walk the student to the toy area and set the stage for imaginative play. For example, pretend a pool noodle is a friendly dolphin that loves to swim. Have the student name all the items and create a specific way each toy likes to move in the water. For example, take a rubber frog and say, "This is Freddy the froggy, and he likes to jump in water like this." Then demonstrate the movement on the deck, out of the water (maybe in a pail or basin of water). As each toy plays its imaginative part, move it a little closer to the pool entry.

Student Directions
The student sits on the deck, responds to requests to play with toys, get toys wet, and moves closer to the pool entry point. The activity ends when the student becomes comfortable enough to sit on the pool's edge or enter the water or the session ends. More work on this activity may be needed at the next session.

Wake Up! It's Gardening Time

Skill 1.1—Play With Toys on the Pool Deck

Equipment
Watering cans, plastic flowers, several inexpensive rubber bath mats

Preparation
Set a plastic watering can and a few sets of plastic flowers on the pool deck. Rubber bath mats can be used to create pathways among the flowers.

Formation
The student is sitting on the pool deck facing the instructor in a safe, low-traffic area of the pool deck that is close to a pool entry point.

Instructor Directions

The student feels each object before starting the activity. Then she waters each set of flowers. Pretend with the student that your lower bodies are the roots of trees that, like any other plants, need water.

Student Directions

The student feels each object before starting the activity. Then she waters the flowers by moving to each set. In addition, she waters her legs and feet (and yours), pretending to water the roots of an imaginary tree.

Watering Time!

Skill 1.2—Sit on the Edge of the Pool With Feet in the Water

Equipment

Plastic watering cans, pool toys, several inexpensive rubber bath mats

Preparation

Put several bath mats on the pool edge for the student to sit on to keep from slipping. Have a small plastic watering can and several sets of plastic flowers standing in the pool gutter or at the edge of the pool.

Formation

The student sits on the edge of the pool with his lower body (feet) in the water so he can reach the water to refill the watering can.

Instructor Directions

Demonstrate filling up the watering can and watering the flowers; then ask the student to pick up one of the watering cans, dip it in the water, and water some of the flowers in the gutter or at the edge of the pool, and maybe his own feet! If the student is not able to refill the can, you can help him.

Student Directions

The student dips the watering can into pool and waters the flowers while hanging his legs over the side of the pool. The purpose of this game is to motivate the student to have his lower body close to the water and get a little wet.

Mud Bath

Skill 1.3—Sit on the Edge of the Pool With Feet in the Water and Splash

Equipment

None

Preparation

Before starting this activity, create a fun story about encountering a pile of mud during an adventure in the forest.

Formation

The student sits on the edge of the pool with her feet in the water.

Instructor Directions

Tell a story about being together in the forest and encountering a big pile of mud. Pretend the pool water is thick mud. With the student, cover every inch of your body with mud (pool water) to hide from the mud creatures.

Student Directions

Following your story, the student uses her hands to scoop water and rub it all over her body, pretending it is mud. The activity ends when she is wet.

Color Me Blue

Skill 1.3—Sit on the Edge of the Pool With Feet in the Water and Splash

Equipment

Soft unused paintbrushes, beach sand pails, poly spots (typically a round, vinyl, colored marker)

Preparation

Place a poly spot at the edge of the pool with a paintbrush in a beach pail next to it.

Formation

The student sits on the poly spot on the side of the pool with her feet and legs over the side.

Instructor Directions

Ask the student what her favorite color is, and then tell her the pool is a huge bucket of that color paint. Ask her to use the bucket to scoop up some paint and paint the deck, herself, you, and the ladder!

Student Directions

The student tells you her favorite color. Then she fills the bucket and pretends to paint various body parts and things in the environment.

Shower Hour 1

Skill 1.4—Sit on the Edge of the Pool and Kick Feet in the Water

Equipment

Small beach ball

Preparation

Place a small beach ball in the water near where you are standing facing the student.

Formation

The student sits on the edge of the pool with his legs hanging over the edge and his feet in the water.

Instructor Directions

Standing in the water, face the student and tell him that you need a good shower with a lot of water!

Student Directions

The student kicks as hard as possible so you can shower. A small beach ball in front of him that he can kick may motivate him to kick harder.

Red Light, Green Light

Skill 1.4—Sit on the Edge of the Pool and Kick Feet in the Water

Equipment

None

Preparation

This is a group activity that works as a warm-up for a lesson.

Formation

The students sit on the edge of the pool with their feet in the water. The instructor is in the water facing the students.

Instructor Directions

Explain the three commands in this game: red light, yellow light, and green light. Red light means stop kicking or splashing (make sure to introduce this one first so you always have a stop signal!), yellow light means kick lightly (a light bubble like boiling water), and green light means kick as hard as you can. In the beginning you call out the commands; later, have the students take turns calling.

Student Directions

The students listen for your call and kick at the appropriate intensity. This activity ends when the students are sufficiently warmed up and pretty wet from the splashing.

Monkey Business

Skill 1.5—Climb Down the Ladder Into Chest-Deep Water

Equipment

Ladder in the pool

Preparation

Make sure no other classes are going on right by the ladder.

Formation

The student sits on the deck near the ladder facing the instructor.

Instructor Directions

Set the stage for this game with a story of monkeys who love to climb. Explain that monkeys like to climb around and explore the pool, but they always make sure they are safe and careful. To do this, they need to climb down the ladder slowly. Demonstrate being curious and going down the ladder slowly.

Student Directions

Now it is the student's turn to be like a monkey. Holding on to the ladder, the student uses her legs and arms to climb down the ladder trying to get her chest wet. In a sloped pool, walk backward into the pool with the student until her chest is wet.

Up and Down

Skill 1.6—Climb up the Ladder to Get Out of the Pool

Equipment

None

Preparation

Bring some math problems and make sure the area of the ladder is clear of other groups.

Formation

The instructor stands in the pool next to the ladder while the student stands in the pool facing the ladder from 5 feet (1.5 m) away. This should be done at waist-deep or chest-deep water.

Instructor Directions

Give the student a math problem with an answer that is a single-digit number (e.g., 2 plus 2). After responding with a number, the student takes that number of steps toward the ladder.

Student Directions

The student responds to your math problem. If he provides the correct answer, he takes that number of steps forward (the number from the correct answer). However, if he provides the incorrect answer, he takes that number of steps back (the number from the incorrect answer). The goal is for the student to eventually climb the ladder by providing correct answers. The activity ends when the student has made it to the top of the ladder.

Locomotor Skills in the Pool

Having students perform locomotor skills (such as walking, running, and jumping) in the water is a great way to introduce them to the shallow end of the pool. In addition, performing locomotor skills in the pool can be a great exercise for improving cardiorespiratory endurance and can help people stay in shape after an injury.

Cues

- High knees
- Opposite arm with opposite leg
- Quick feet

Differentiation

- A family member or assistant can provide support to students with balance issues or those who have difficulty staying focused.
- Students who cannot run can walk.
- Students who cannot run can perform the skill by holding on to the edge of the pool.
- Those with lower-body disabilities can use a jog belt or use their hands to jog.
- For those with lower-body disabilities, a swim stroke using flotation can be substituted for a locomotor skill.

Gutterball

Skill 1.7—Walk at Least 12 Yards Holding the Pool Gutter or Edge

Equipment

Many small balls that can fit into the gutter (at least five per student)

Preparation

Place five or more balls for each student in the gutters 12 yards from the start position. If the pool does not have a gutter, you can use a plastic floating bowl to hold the balls.

In Gutterball, the instructor makes sure the students are holding the gutter or edge of the pool and provides assistance as needed.

Formation

The students are in two groups facing the wall while holding the gutter or the edge of the pool. Balls are placed between the two groups.

Instructor Directions

The goal of this game is for students to walk 12 yards or more along the pool edge, grab a ball, and bring it back to their side; they try to get as many balls as possible to their side of the wall before you say, "Stop." Demonstrate walking from one spot in the pool to the other, grabbing a ball, and putting it back at your home base on the deck. Start the activity by saying "Go"; then have one student from each team go at a time. Say "Stop" when all of the balls are gone.

Student Directions

When you say, "Go," the students hold the gutter or edge of the pool and walk to the place where their balls are located, retrieve one ball, and bring it back to their starting spot. They try to retrieve as many balls as possible.

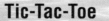

Water Dancing

Skill 1.8—Walk in Chest-Deep Water at Least 12 Yards Holding the Instructor's Hand

Equipment

Music player with fun music

Preparation

Have music on when the game begins.

Formation

The student and the instructor are in chest-deep water facing each other and holding hands.

Instructor Directions

Just as in dancing, count 1, 2, 3, 4, 5, 6, 7, 8 evenly to keep a beat. Start by walking backward as the student walks forward. Choices of music might include rock, salsa, swing, or merengue.

Student Directions

The student holds your hands and pretends she is dancing by walking at least 12 yards to a beat.

Tic-Tac-Toe

Skill 1.9—Walk Across the Pool Independently

Equipment

Tic-tac-toe board, X and O pieces (pool noodle pieces and water rings can be used as pieces)

Preparation

Place a tic-tac-toe board on the deck on one side of the pool and two types of pieces (representing Xs and Os) on the deck of the other side of the pool (at least four of each type).

Formation

Two players start on the side where the pieces are laid out. One person has Xs and the other has Os.

Instructor Directions

Explain to the students that they will take one of their game pieces and walk to the other side of the pool and place it on the tic-tac-toe board. Students take turns placing the pieces on the board. They continue to go back and forth until there are no more pieces left; then they see who has won the game. Players should keep going until all the pieces are used, even if someone wins early in the game.

Student Directions

Students walk back and forth 12 yards at a time transporting the tic-tac-toe pieces to the other side to play the game.

Shallow End Tag

Skill 1.10—Run Across the Pool Independently

Equipment

Pool noodle, 10 tall traffic cones

Preparation

In waist- to chest-deep water, place 10 tall traffic cones on the bottom of the pool to form a small circle, no more than 3 feet (1 m) away from the side of the pool.

Formation

Students are in waist- to chest-deep water scattered around the small circle of cones, ready to run clockwise. The instructor sits at the pool edge with a long foam pool noodle facing the circle.

Instructor Directions

Demonstrate running in a circle around the underwater cones, staying close to the cones. Explain to the students that they must run around the cones quickly to avoid being tagged by the instructor's foam pool noodle. If the students are tagged, they must run to the end of the pool and back to get back into the circle. Play this for one minute and reverse directions of the running. Make this a timed event with a rest period every two minutes. This game works on cardiorespiratory fitness, muscular strength, and endurance.

Student Directions

Students run in a clockwise direction around a circle of underwater cones, making sure they stay close to the cones. They should run quickly when they come near you while you try to tag them with the foam pool noodle. They will run in the opposite direction around the cones at your cue. If the students are tagged, they will run to the end of the pool and back to get back into the circle.

Blob Tag

Skill 1.10—Run Across the Pool Independently

Equipment
None

Preparation
None

Formation
Students are spread out around the shallow end of the pool.

Instructor Directions
Explain and demonstrate that students who are tagged link arms with the tagger and become part of the blob that tries to tag others.

Student Directions
One student is the tagger, and the other students flee to avoid getting tagged. Students who are tagged link arms with the tagger, forming a blob. As more people get tagged, the blob becomes bigger. The game continues until everyone is tagged. Students must stay linked while tagging.

Pot of Gold

Skill 1.10—Run Across the Pool Independently

Equipment
Item that serves as a pot for the gold (for example, a bucket), laminated shamrock, laminated gold coins

Preparation
Cut one large shamrock out of green paper and laminate. Cut large gold circles and laminate to act as coins (one per student, plus extra to keep at the starting side of the pool). Decorate a bucket to serve as a pot of gold.

Formation
Students are on one side of the pool, each holding a gold coin. The instructor is sitting on the edge of the pool behind the students, holding the shamrock.

Instructor Directions
Explain to the students that this is a tag game in which they have to run through the water from one side of the pool to the other without getting tagged with the

shamrock by the instructor. Students will be running from the tagger and will hold a gold coin that they must give up if they are tagged. Remind students that when tagged, they must give up their gold. The goal is for the students to reach the pot without being tagged so that they can place their gold coin in the pot.

Student Directions

Students run from one side of the pool to the other to place a gold coin in the pot of gold without getting tagged with the shamrock by the instructor. If tagged, they must give the instructor their coin and then go safely to the beginning to receive another coin to try to get into the pot of gold. If they are successful placing a coin into the pot of gold, they go back to the beginning to retrieve another coin. At the end of one or two minutes, the instructor adds up the coins collected in the pot.

Washing Machine

Skill 1.11—Turn in a Circle in Chest-Deep Water

Equipment

Five to ten washcloths, some objects (sponges) to help each washcloth float, poly spots (one per student)

Preparation

Place several washcloths over large sponges that are floating in the pool. Put poly spots on the bottom of the pool in a circle in chest-deep water.

Formation

The students stand in chest-deep water in a circle, one per poly spot.

Instructor Directions

Ask the students if they have seen how the clothes spin inside a watching machine. Put several of the floating washcloths in the center of the circle and have the students spin around them to the right and then to the left to wash the clothes. You can provide support by joining the circle and having the students hold hands as they move clockwise and then counterclockwise.

Student Directions

Students stand in a circle and then rotate to the right or left as you call out directions.

Twizzle

Skill 1.11—Turn in a Circle in Chest-Deep Water

Equipment

None

Preparation

None

Formation

Students stand in a circle in chest-deep water.

Instructor Directions

Explain the game and demonstrate what each command means (see Student Directions). Begin with easy commands such as Stop and Go until the students are familiar with the game.

Student Directions

Students start in a circle and follow your commands. The commands are as follows:

- Go—Move forward or walk.
- Stop—Stop where you are.
- Turn—Turn on your toes 180 degrees and face the opposite direction.
- Jump—Jump up and turn 180 degrees to face the opposite direction.
- Twizzle—Jump in the air and spin 360 degrees and land facing the same direction.

Rocket Ship 1

Skill 1.12—Jump Three Times Holding the Instructor's Hand

Equipment

None

Preparation

None

Formation

The student and the instructor face each other in waist-deep or chest-deep water.

Instructor Directions

Hold the student's hand for three jumps (under the water to the chin). Then give the student a little extra boost to take off as high as appropriate. Hold both of the student's hands.

Student Directions

It's time to be a rocket ship! The rocket ship must prepare three rocket boosters (i.e., bob three times) before takeoff. The student goes down to chin depth three times and then jumps as high as possible.

The student rockets up out of the water. If the student prefers, the instructor can hold the student by the hands or the waist.

Popcorn

Skill 1.13—Jump Three Times Independently

Equipment
Watering can or bucket

Preparation
None

Formation
Students are scattered in chest-deep water far enough apart that they do not jump into each other.

Instructor Directions
Tell the students that they are going to the movie theater and will buy some delicious popcorn. Pour popcorn oil (water) on the students' heads and explain that when the water is poured on their heads, they are ready to pop.

Student Directions
When the water is poured on their heads, the students pop (jump up and down) in various directions at least three times pretending to be popcorn.

Who's at the Zoo?

Skill 1.14—Jump Continuously in Chest-Deep Water for at Least 12 Yards Independently

Equipment
None

Preparation
Think of various zoo animals to present to the class; put a large cone 12 yards away underwater as an end point.

Formation
Students line up in waist- to chest-deep water with their backs against the pool wall.

Instructor Directions
Ask the students, "What animals jump with two feet?" When the students answer, tell them to jump with two feet like that animal to the designated spot 12 yards away.

Student Directions
Students call out the names of animals that can jump with two feet. Then they jump across the pool like those animals.

Can You Balance?

Skill 1.15—Hop Three Times on the Preferred Foot, Holding the Instructor's Hand

Equipment
Three poly spots

Preparation
Place three poly spots close together (2 ft, or 61 cm, apart) on the bottom of the pool in chest-deep water.

Formation
The student and the instructor are in waist-deep water.

Instructor Directions
Tell the student to stand on a poly spot with her preferred foot and see how long she can stay balanced. Then have her try her nonpreferred foot. Then challenge her to hop at least three times from one poly spot to another while holding your hand.

Student Directions
The student balances on her preferred foot and then her nonpreferred foot, and then hops on one foot from one poly spot to another three times while holding your hand.

Water Triple Hop

Skill 1.16—Hop Three Times on the Preferred Foot Independently

Equipment
Three sinkable objects between 3 and 4 inches in height

Preparation
Place three objects in the bottom of the pool in waist- or chest-deep water in a line about 12 inches (30 cm) apart.

Formation
The instructor is beside the student, who is facing the area of the sinkable objects. They are 12 inches (30 cm) away from the first object.

Instructor Directions
Describe and demonstrate walking to the objects and hopping over each one on your preferred foot. Then have the student do the same while you spot him in case he falls over.

Student Directions
The student walks toward the objects and then hops with his preferred foot while trying to maintain his balance.

Water Familiarization and Blowing Bubbles

Water familiarization is the first step for beginner swimmers. It includes introducing the student to water and breathing techniques such as blowing bubbles. Blowing air out with pursed lips is a lead-up skill to the rhythmic breathing used in swim strokes. By practicing the motion of blowing air, a ping-pong ball, and then bubbles at and just below the surface, students progress toward the skills of bobbing and rhythmic breathing required for safe swim stroke techniques.

Cues

- Blow air from your mouth or cheeks.
- Pretend you are blowing out a candle.
- Don't drink the water.
- Say "Mmmmmmmmm."

Differentiation

- Provide positive feedback for any approximation of the skill (encouragement).
- Allow students with visual impairments to place a hand in front of your mouth so they can feel the air coming out.
- Repeat the directions and provide extra demonstrations for those who are having trouble understanding the activities.
- Keep the pool area free of distractions, splashing, and loud noises for those who have startle reflex tendencies.

Morning Routine

Skill 1.17—Pretend to Wash the Face With Water

Equipment

Bell, washcloths (one per student)

Preparation

Gather as many washcloths as there are students.

Formation

Students are standing against the wall in the shallow end, facing the instructor, who is in the water 10 feet (3 m) away.

Instructor Directions

Explain that the students will pretend to go through their morning routine of stretching, washing up, and so on. Demonstrate the motions. Remind them that this is just pretend and that they should not actually brush their teeth with the water.

Student Directions

Students pretend to go through their morning routines while in the water. When a bell rings, they get up and stretch and pretend to brush their teeth and hair and wash their faces with washcloths.

Where the Wind Blows

Skill 1.18—Blow a Ping-Pong Ball on the Water Surface

Equipment

Ping-pong balls (one per student)

Preparation

None

Formation

Students stand with their backs to the pool wall in shallow water (about waist to chest deep).

Instructor Directions

Give each student a ping-pong ball and tell them not to put them in their mouths. Demonstrate blowing a ping-pong ball on the water surface. Give commands such as "The wind is blowing left" and "The wind is blowing right." Keep repeating commands (right, center, and left) until the students reach you. Then have them each turn around and blow the ball back to the wall.

Student Directions

On your signal, each student blows a ping-pong ball across the surface of the water toward the left, right, or center depending on which way you say the wind is blowing. After they have reached you, they each turn around and blow the ball back to the wall.

Ping-Pong Water Soccer

Skill 1.18—Blow a Ping-Pong Ball on the Water Surface

Equipment

Ping-pong balls, two hula hoops

Preparation

Place two hula hoops in the water with two ping-pong balls the same distance away from each hoop.

Formation

Students are paired according to their skill levels and stand facing their partners from 3 feet (1 m) away. A hula hoop is behind each student, and two different colored ping-pong balls are between the students in each pair.

Instructor Directions

Demonstrate blowing a ping-pong ball into a hoop; then tell the students to blow their ping-pong balls into the hula hoop behind their partners to score a goal. For health reasons, no defense should be played (so students don't blow into each other's faces); instead, students attempt to score before their partners do. Have them repeat as many times as you want.

Student Directions

Students are in pairs blowing ping-pong balls across the surface of the water into their opponents' hoops to try to score before their opponents do. They may not use their hands or any other body part to move their balls.

Talk to the Fishy

Skill 1.19—Blow Bubbles on the Water Surface

Equipment

Large submersible plastic fish, hula hoops

Preparation

Have a hula hoop floating on the water in chest-deep water. Submerge the plastic fish so that it is in the middle of the floating hoop.

Formation

Students stand in a circle around the hula hoop.

Instructor Directions

Explain to the students that the fish speaks a special bubble language. To talk to the fish, they need to blow bubbles in the water. Demonstrate blowing bubbles with your mouth inside the hoop.

Student Directions

The students submerge their heads until their lips are covered with water. Then, they pretend to talk to the fish by blowing bubbles.

Water Limbo

Skill 1.20—Place the Face in the Water While Holding the Gutter or Pool Edge

Equipment

Pool noodles

Preparation

Prop one end of a pool noodle on the pool gutter or edge 5 feet (1.5 m) in front of the line of students.

Formation

Students stand in a straight line in the shallow water, holding the gutter or the edge of the pool with their right hands and facing the instructor, who has the limbo stick (noodle).

Instructor Directions

Explain that the students should hold the wall with one hand while walking toward you. When they get to the limbo stick (noodle), they place their faces in the water as they walk under the limbo stick. When all of the students have gone under the limbo stick, they reverse directions and, holding the wall with their other hands, repeat the activity. How low can they go? Eventually, drop the limbo stick on the water, so students have to walk or move underwater.

Student Directions

The students walk under the limbo stick with their faces in the water.

Pop-Up Underwater Ball

Skill 1.21—Place the Face in the Water Without Holding on to Anything

Equipment

Small beach ball (at least 6 in., or 15 cm, in diameter)

Preparation

Blow up the beach ball.

Formation

Students are scattered around the shallow water far enough apart that they will not bump into each other.

Instructor Directions

Show the students how a ball explodes out of the water after you push it underwater. Then ask them to pretend to be balls and mimic the motion while you push the ball under again. When you say, "Go," the students place their faces underwater and immediately jump up as you release the ball.

Student Directions

Students stand in shallow water and, when you push the beach ball underwater and it pops up, they bend their knees, submerge a bit underwater, and then jump up.

Pop-Up Underwater Ball is a fun way to introduce a student to getting her entire body wet.

Listening to the Fishes

Skill 1.22—Blow Bubbles, Breathe, and Blow Bubbles

Equipment
None

Preparation
None

Formation
Students are in chest-deep water facing the instructor.

Instructor Directions
Say, "We can talk to the fishes, and then it's time for them to talk to us." Demonstrate blowing bubbles with your face in the water (talking to the fishes), and then turning your head to the side with your ear in the water (listening to the fishes). Have the students do the same; when their ears are in the water, say a short, easy word underwater to see if they can hear it. To keep things interesting, ask them to repeat what the fish (you) just said. Help position their heads, if needed.

Student Directions
Students blow bubbles, with as much of their faces in the water as possible, and then turn their faces to the side and place their ears in the water so they can listen to what the fishes have to say.

Happy Birthday

An instructor holds a diving stick underwater while the swimmer pretends it is a birthday candle she needs to blow out.

Skill 1.23—Blow Bubbles, Breathe, and Blow Bubbles Three Times in a Row

Equipment
Three flexible diving sticks or large candles

Preparation
None

Formation
Students are in a semicircle in chest-deep water facing the instructor from 3 feet (1 m) away.

Instructor Directions
Explain that the diving sticks are special birthday candles that can go underwater! Hold them underwater and put your face in the water to blow out one candle. Then take a breath to the side and blow out another candle; do this again until you have blown out all three candles. Then ask the students to do the same.

Student Directions

The students start by placing their faces to the side with their ears in the water. After singing "Happy Birthday," they rotate their faces underwater and blow bubbles (to blow out one candle). They then turn to the side, take a breath, and turn to blow out another candle, and then the final one.

Moving Underwater

It is very common for beginner swimmers to be afraid to go underwater. Therefore, you need to introduce underwater activities when students are developmentally ready.

Cues

- Keep your eyes open.
- Blow your bubbles.
- Lower yourself down.
- Push the water up.

Differentiation

- For students with visual impairments, place sinking objects under their feet to begin the activity.
- Put sinkable objects on a plastic crate at the bottom of the pool for those students who cannot submerge their bodies all the way.
- Hold the student by the waist to assist her on the way down and on the way up.
- Use a swim mask or goggles for beginner students to explore underwater.

Ringer

Skill 1.24—Pick Up a Ring (or Other Object) From the Bottom of the Pool

Equipment

Sinkable pool rings, ring toss target

Preparation

Gather at least two sinkable rings per student and scatter them around the shallow end.

Formation

Students stand in a large circle around the shallow end with all the rings in the middle of the circle.

Instructor Directions

Explain and demonstrate how to get to the bottom of the pool by taking a breath, submerging, pushing water up to the surface with your hands, opening your eyes, and grabbing a ring. Call out "Ringer" to begin the activity. Tell the students that when they have a ring, they should toss it to the ring toss target that is close to the wall. If the ring does not make it onto the stick, it becomes part of the game again by sinking to the bottom. Make sure the ring toss stick is not near the students who are submerging.

Student Directions

Students practice submerging, blowing bubbles, grabbing rings off the pool floor in the shallow end, and tossing them onto the ring toss stick.

LEVEL

2

Developing Initial Skills

Modified Texas Woman's University Aquatic Assessment: Level 2

Student's name: _____   Instructor's name: _____

Student's date of birth: _____   Date: _____

Page number	Skill number	Skill description	Yes	No	Comments
58	2.1	Bob in chest-deep water once with instructor's help			
60	2.2	Bob once holding the gutter or pool edge			
61	2.3	Bob once independently			
62	2.4	Bob five consecutive times in chest-deep water independently			
64	2.5	Float on front with face in water with instructor's help for three seconds			
67	2.6	Front flutter kick while being towed 12 yards by the instructor while blowing bubbles			
69	2.7	Spin in a circle without touching the bottom of the pool			
70	2.8	Float on front with instructor's help for three seconds while blowing bubbles and recover to a stand			
71	2.9	Float on front while holding the pool gutter or edge for three seconds while blowing bubbles and recover to a stand			
72	2.10	Float on front independently for three seconds while blowing bubbles and recover to a stand			
72	2.11	Float on front for five seconds independently			
73	2.12	Float on front for three seconds while blowing bubbles and recover to a stand independently			
73	2.13	Float on back with instructor support			

Page number	Skill number	Skill description	Yes	No	Comments
75	2.14	Float on back and recover to a stand with instructor's help			
76	2.15	Float on back and recover to a stand with one hand on the pool gutter or edge			
77	2.16	Float on back and recover to a stand independently			
78	2.17	Float on back for five seconds independently			
80	2.18	Flutter kick on back while being towed 12 yards by the instructor			
82	2.19	Get out of the water without a ladder with instructor support			
83	2.20	Get out of the water without a ladder independently			
84	2.21	Jump into chest-deep water from a sitting position, holding the instructor's hand			
85	2.22	Jump into chest-deep water from a standing position, holding the instructor's hand			
86	2.23	Jump into chest-deep water independently			
87	2.24	Hang on to the pool gutter or edge in deep water, submerge the whole body, and recover to the surface			

General comments:

Modified from Texas Woman's University Aquatic Assessment.

From M. Lepore, L. Columna, and L. Friedlander Litzner, 2015, *Assessments and activities for teaching swimming* (Champaign, IL: Human Kinetics).

This level focuses on basic aquatic activities to develop the skills for level 2 of the Modified TWU Aquatic Assessment. As in level 1, we recommend that you conduct a thorough assessment to determine your students' level of performance and to discover what skills you need to teach. You may find that a student possesses skills in several levels and might need to complete level 1 before moving on to level 2. All students need the fundamentals to progress in the swim levels. Level 2 includes 24 swim skills.

You may have students in your group who have disabilities that prevent them from completing a skill as described. In this case, try to provide an accommodation to help them achieve the skill or modify the skill. If the skill is simply not appropriate (e.g., kicking for someone with lower-body paralysis), write *N/A* (not applicable) on the assessment form, explain why the skill is not applicable, and move on.

The key at this level is to be patient and provide a safe environment with fun experiences that are developmentally appropriate. You don't need to do all the activities in this chapter; make your choices based on the age and ability level of the student. As much as possible, involve the student in the process of identifying where to start and what activities to do.

The activities in this level are general ideas for making the aquatic experience fun. Feel free to safely modify any of them and to add some of your own.

Bobbing

Bobbing involves taking a breath, closing the mouth, submerging the body by bending the knees at a 90-degree angle to the floor, blowing all the air out through the mouth and nose, and straightening the knees to pop up out of the water (see figure L2.1). This is typically done repeatedly. Bobbing can be used to warm up the body; practice breath control; and increase balance, leg strength, and endurance.

Cues
- Breath in; hold your breath.
- Bend your knees 90 degree when going underwater.
- Blow bubbles.
- Stay straight as an arrow.
- Jump up; then breathe in.

Differentiation
- Allow students with mobility challenges to use an in-water plastic chair or use the wall near the stairs to maneuver down the ladder using their hands.
- Provide physical support for those who need it.
- Provide a tactile model (adult or other child demonstrates the action and student appropriately feels or touches the body movement) for students who are visually impaired or any student who needs additional non-visual instruction.

Figure L2.1   The swimmer *(a)* submerges vertically under water, blowing out bubbles, to begin bobbing and *(b)* pops up out of the water after blowing bubbles.

- Provide physical support if needed, remind students where they are supposed to be, and use poly spots to designate the area to stay within.
- For students who cannot jump up or reach the bottom of the pool, use a table or a platform that can submerge underwater.
- Have students without mobility in the lower extremities use one hand to hold on to something.
- Allow students who cannot hold their breath for a long enough period of time (five seconds) to use a mask and snorkel.
- Count out loud to motivate students and help them focus.
- Let students feel where the noodle is if they cannot see it.
- Use sign language for counting if needed.
- If the student cannot submerge all the way under during the initial stages of learning to bob, encourage the student to submerge to chin level, then progress to the mouth level, then nose level.

I See, You Saw

Skill 2.1—Bob in Chest-Deep Water Once With Instructor's Help

Equipment
None

Preparation
This is an introductory activity to get the student comfortable with moving up and down in the water. You can have a list of other phrases besides *see-saw* and allow the student to pick the one he wants to say.

Formation
The student and the instructor (or other student) face each other in chest-deep water, holding hands.

Instructor Directions
You will start the game by saying your word. For example, if your word is *see*, you submerge in the water, pop up, and say "See." Next, the student submerges, pops up, and says "Saw." Other options for phrases include *ice cream, Sponge Bob, good morning,* and *blast off.*

Student Directions
The student waits until you have popped back up and said "See" before submerging, popping up, and saying "Saw." Students may submerge to chin level, then progress to mouth level, then nose level.

Swimmers play the see-saw game to practice bobbing and breath control with a friend or the instructor.

Rocket Ship 2

Skill 2.1—Bob in Chest-Deep Water Once With Instructor's Help

Equipment
None

Preparation
None

Formation
The student and the instructor face each other in chest-deep water, holding hands.

Instructor Directions
Hold the student's hand while bobbing once; then, with a little extra boost from you, the student can take off as high as appropriate. Make sure you hold both hands of the student. You can say, "It's time to be a rocket ship!" The rocket ship can prepare five rocket boosters (bob to chin level five times) before full submersion.

Student Directions
The student bobs once and then jumps as high as possible with your support.

Ring Around the Rosie

Skill 2.1—Bob in Chest-Deep Water Once With Instructor's Help

Equipment
None

Preparation
Learn the lyrics of the song "Ring Around the Rosie," or select any other song appropriate for young students; modify for older students.

Formation
The student and the instructor are facing each other in chest-deep water and holding hands; others can join to make a small circle.

Instructor Directions
Demonstrate traveling clockwise to create a mini whirlpool while singing, "Ring around the rosie, come and pick some posies, picking, picking, we all fall down." Explain that when you get to the line "we all fall down," everyone dunks underwater as far as they feel comfortable and blows bubbles.

Student Directions
Students travel clockwise forming a mini whirlpool while singing the song "Ring Around the Rosie." When they come to the line "we all fall down," they dunk themselves underwater as far as they are comfortable and blow bubbles.

Magic Spot

Skill 2.2—Bob Once Holding the Gutter or Pool Edge

Equipment

Poly spots (one per student) or any other space marker that is flat, sinkable, and waterproof

Preparation

Place poly spots or markers on the bottom of the pool within 2 feet (61 cm) of the wall where students are holding the gutter or pool edge.

Formation

Each student faces and holds the gutter or pool edge in chest-deep water while standing on a poly spot.

Instructor Directions

Explain that the poly spot or marker is each student's own mini trampoline. Have them bob under water, blow bubbles, and then jump on the spot and see how high they can go.

Student Directions

The student bobs under water, jumps as high as possible, and lands on the poly spot or marker.

Dolphin Jump

Skill 2.2—Bob Once Holding the Gutter or Pool Edge

Equipment

Poly spot or flat sinkable marker, hula hoop

Preparation

Put a poly spot or a flat marker on the bottom of the pool under the student. Have a hula hoop ready. This activity helps the student practice when to breathe in and when to breathe out while bobbing.

Formation

The student holds the gutter or pool edge with one hand (in chest-deep water) above where the poly spot or marker is on the bottom of the pool. The instructor holds a hula hoop horizontally about 6 inches (15 cm) above the student's head.

Instructor Directions

Explain that in a sea life show, the dolphins are taught to jump through a hoop; they take a breath while up in the hoop and blow bubbles while underwater. Blow a whistle or say the word "Go" to signal the student to jump up through the hoop and take a breath of air. Explain that she will bend her knees upon landing, and when her mouth goes underwater, she should breathe out, or blow bubbles.

Student Directions

When the student hears the whistle or the word "Go," she jumps up so her head goes through the hoop, takes a deep breath, and then bends her knees upon landing. When water hits her mouth, she breathes out, making bubbles.

Fun With Tigger

Skill 2.2—Bob Once Holding the Gutter or Pool Edge

Equipment

Cones; laminated pictures of Winnie-the-Pooh, Tigger, and Piglet, or other characters or objects motivating to the student

Preparation

Laminate various photos of Winnie-the-Pooh and friends, especially Tigger. If the student is not interested in these characters, find out what he is interested in. If he is interested in animals (kangaroos or frogs), cartoons, or a certain basketball player, create a scenario in which he pretends to be like them. Use appropriate props such as pictures or a basketball hoop.

Formation

The student is standing in chest-deep water.

Instructor Directions

Explain to the student that he will jump like Tigger and bob between each jump. Tape pictures of Pooh, Piglet, and Eeyore to cones and place them about 3 feet (1 m) apart around the pool gutter or edge, so Tigger can bob over to say hello! Have photos brailled, substitute other movements, or use minimal flotation if necessary.

Student Directions

On your signal, the student jumps and bobs independently (while holding the pool gutter or edge) like Tigger to say hello to pictures of Pooh, Piglet, and Eeyore around the pool area.

How High

Skill 2.3—Bob Once Independently

Equipment

Pool noodle with markings to designate length such as inches or centimeters

Preparation

Make a pool noodle into a ruler to mark how high the student can jump on the fifth bob.

The instructor can introduce the student to How High in waist-deep water and then progress to chest-deep water when the student is comfortable.

Formation

Both the student and the instructor are in chest-deep water facing each other. The instructor is holding the pool noodle between them straight up with one end of the noodle on the water surface.

Instructor Directions

While in the pool, hold the ruler (pool noodle) with one hand and ask the student to bob under the water and then jump as high as she can to touch the ruler. Explain that she should jump higher and higher each time. Mark off her highest jump, and then see if she can jump higher later in the class. Use this to mark the student's progress over time as well.

Student Directions

When you say "Go," the student jumps and touches her hand to the pool noodle to measure her jump. She tries to jump higher each time.

Head Start

Skill 2.4—Bob Five Consecutive Times in Chest-Deep Water Independently

Equipment

Pool noodle

Preparation

None

Formation

The student and the instructor are in chest-deep water next to each other.

Instructor Directions

Hold a pool noodle 6 inches (15 cm) over the student's head. Tell her to bob five times and try to have her head hit the noodle as she pops up out of the water (make sure to explain that the farther down she goes, the higher she will be able to jump).

Student Directions

On your signal, the student bobs five times and tries to have her head hit the noodle as she pops up out of the water.

In the activity Head Start, the instructor lifts the pool noodle higher after each successful attempt.

Floating With Support

Floating involves the ability to stay suspended in the water in a relatively horizontal position (on the front or on the back) with minimal to no movement. The most basic way to float is to extend all appendages outward to create a large, flat surface area and to lift the feet off the bottom of the pool. Your support of the student should consist mainly of supporting the torso and head (see figure L2.2).

Figure L2.2   One way to provide support to a swimmer floating on his back is to have the swimmer rest his head on the instructor's shoulder.

Cues for the Back Float

- Head back
- Ears in water
- Chin up
- Arms and legs out
- Belly up

Cues for the Front Float

- Nose toward the floor
- Arms and legs out
- Belly down

Differentiation

- Provide support under the back and head; use several pool noodles and remove one at a time as the student progresses.
- Provide flotation under a body part that is denser than the others.
- Let the student hold floating barbells in each hand for support or have one under each armpit.
- Use inexpensive blow-up rafts somewhat deflated for support.

Freeze Frame on Front

Skill 2.5—Float on Front With Face in Water With Instructor's Help for Three Seconds

Equipment
Floating foam mat

Preparation
None

Formation
The student and the instructor are in chest-deep water facing each other with a floating foam mat between them.

A swimmer lies on her front like a starfish in preparation for floating independently.

Instructor Directions

Have the student lie on the mat on her belly like a starfish. She can practice this out of the pool first. You can create a diagram of the floating position on the mat with a drawing or picture of a starfish, Superman, the sun, or the letter X. Use this opportunity to correctly position the student. Adjust her arms or legs and remind her of the correct head position.

Student Directions

The student climbs onto the mat and lies on her belly like a starfish or any other formation pictured on the mat.

I Wanna Be the Sun

Skill 2.5—Float on Front With Face in Water With Instructor's Help for Three Seconds

Equipment

Pool noodle

Preparation

Cut a regular-size pool noodle into thirds.

Formation

The student and the instructor are in chest-deep water facing each other with pool noodle pieces nearby.

Instructor Directions

Explain to the student that she is going to be the sun and that her arms and legs will be the rays of the sun, extending out to warm up the water. Demonstrate the front float with your arms and legs spread out away from your body; then ask the student to extend her legs and arms as far as possible and try to stay on top of

A swimmer spreads her arms and legs as far as she can, like rays of the sun.

the water. She can hold on to the small noodle bits at first, and you can take them away one by one. Support at the waist may be needed.

Student Directions

The student lies on her belly (prone position) and holds two small noodle pieces out to the side while spreading her feet out to imitate the rays of the sun. If necessary, an additional noodle can be placed under her hips to help with buoyancy.

Flutter Kicking

Kicking is an important skill for propulsion and stability in the water. The kick should originate at the hip rather than the knee. In the flutter kick, the legs stay relatively straight with a slight knee bend and move up and down in opposition so that the heels just break the surface of the water (see figure L2.3). The torso typically is rolling slightly to the right and left during the front stroke (front crawl) and backstroke, and the feet kick about 10 inches (25 cm) below the surface.

Cues

- Have floppy ankles.
- Splash with your heel (with your knees straight).
- Boil the water.
- Have long legs (to promote limited knee bend).
- Power from your core and kick from your hips.

Differentiation

- If the student does not have mobility of the lower extremities or does not have one or both lower extremities, you can hold his trunk or provide a flotation device such as a pool noodle. The ultimate goals are to encourage independence and for the student to compensate, as much as possible, with his upper body. The student can rotate his body from side to side to create waves.

Figure L2.3   In the flutter kick, the legs should stay relatively straight with a slight knee bend and pointed toes.

- For those with lower-body challenges, use body undulation, the kick used in the butterfly stroke, or arm motions as a substitute for kicks.
- Let students with poor upper-body control lie on a floating pool mat rather than having them hold the wall.
- Provide tactile cues (hands on) for those who cannot see demonstrations.
- Use U.S. Coast Guard–approved PFDs or adult assistance with students who need more support.
- If the student is not able to move her lower body, have her create waves by moving her whole body up and down.
- Use an object with sound localization for students with no vision to move toward.

Treasure Hunt

Skill 2.6—Front Flutter Kick While Being Towed 12 Yards by the Instructor While Blowing Bubbles

Equipment
Kickboard or pool noodle, personalized laminated index cards

Preparation
Create task cards (laminated index cards) with various riddles that lead the student to perform skills and move around the pool. Place these cards around the pool in the gutters or on the pool edge, or hang them from the deck. For a more challenging hunt, spread the cards far apart. For a quicker, basic hunt, keep the cards closer together. The cards can contain simple tasks that must be completed and instructions of where to go next, or more complex tasks such as having to solve a riddle to find out where to go next.

Formation
The student is standing in waist- or chest-deep water close to the instructor, who is standing in the water during the activity.

Instructor Directions
Direct the student to the first card. For example, a riddle on a card that tells the student to flutter kick to the ladder might say this:

Some people use this to climb out of the pool,

but being careful is the golden rule.

Flutter kick on your front or back, it doesn't matter.

Let's go find our next clue at the la—

Help the student figure out that he needs to flutter kick to the ladder, and then tow him on a kickboard or pool noodle while he flutter kicks to the next clue. The clues should be personalized for the level of the student and the pool area.

Student Directions
The student moves using the flutter kick to cards placed around the pool. He should also blow bubbles in the water while being towed.

Obey the Traffic Light

Skill 2.6—Front Flutter Kick While Being Towed 12 Yards by the Instructor While Blowing Bubbles

Equipment
None

Preparation
None

Formation
The students sit on the edge of the pool with their feet in the water. The instructor is in the water facing the students.

Instructor Directions
Explain the three commands in this game: red light means stop kicking and splashing (make sure to introduce this one first so you always have a stop signal!), yellow light means kick lightly (a light bubble, like boiling water), and green light means kick as hard as you can. In the beginning you call out the commands; later, students can take turns calling.

Student Directions
Students listen for the commands and kick at the appropriate intensity with straight legs. The activity ends when you believe they are sufficiently warmed up for the lesson and pretty wet from splashing.

Shower Hour 2

Skill 2.6—Front Flutter Kick While Being Towed 12 Yards by the Instructor While Blowing Bubbles

Equipment
None

Preparation
None

Formation
The student is in chest-deep water, facing the wall of the pool, with the instructor behind her.

Instructor Directions
Demonstrate the technique. Then ask the student to hold the pool wall or gutter, lie in a prone position, and kick. Stand behind her and explain that you need a good shower with a lot of water! During the shower, pretend to be washing up.

Student Directions

The student holds the pool wall or gutter, flutter kicks, and blows bubbles when you ask for a good shower with a lot of water. The student needs to kick as hard as possible so you can get really clean.

Stationary Propulsion

Moving in the water without generating propulsion forward or backward is known as stationary propulsion (treading water). The skill of keeping the head above the water while remaining in one place is important for safety and helps students feel confident and comfortable in the aquatic environment.

Cues

- Kick feet.
- Push water down and out with your hands.
- Push water down and in with your hands.

Differentiation

- If the student does not feel comfortable or does not have adequate control of her body, use a plastic in-water table, chair, or platform to assist her with this task.

Twisty

Skill 2.7—Spin in a Circle Without Touching the Bottom of the Pool

Equipment

Pool noodle, noodle connector (optional), floating toys

Preparation

Bend a foam pool noodle into the shape of an O using a noodle connector (optional).

Formation

The student faces the instructor in chest-deep water inside the circular (connected) pool noodle.

Instructor Directions

Place toys inside the noodle that is around the student. You can hold the noodle in a half circle or use a pool noodle connector to create a smaller circle. Tell the student to try to get the floating toys to spin around him by spinning like a tornado with his feet off the ground.

Student Directions

Once you say "Go," the student lifts his feet off the bottom and uses his arms to spin himself like a tornado in an attempt to get all the floating toys to spin around him.

Floating on the Front and on the Back

Floating involves the ability to stay suspended in the water, in a relatively horizontal position, with minimal to no movement. The most basic way to float is to extend all extremities (arms and legs) outward to create a large, flat surface area and to lift the feet off the bottom of the pool. Your support of students should consist mainly of supporting the torso and head.

Cues for the Back Float

- Head back
- Ears in water
- Chin up
- Arms and legs out
- Belly up

Cues for the Front Float

- Nose toward the floor
- Arms and legs out
- Belly down

Differentiation

- Provide support under the student's back and head.
- Use several pool noodles and remove them one at a time as the student progresses in the ability to float.
- Provide flotation under a body part that is denser than others.
- Let the student hold a floating barbell in each hand or have one under each armpit.
- Use an inexpensive blow-up raft somewhat deflated to give support.
- For students who are deaf, use their preferred mode of communication (sign language or an index card showing the task they have to perform in words or pictures).

Jumping Frogs 1

Skill 2.8—Float on Front With Instructor's Help for Three Seconds While Blowing Bubbles and Recover to a Stand

Equipment

Laminated picture of a lily pad with a frog on it, toy frog

Preparation

Laminate a picture of a lily pad with a frog on it, and have a toy frog on hand.

Formation

Both the student and the instructor are standing in chest-deep water facing each other and holding hands.

Instructor Directions

Show the student the picture of the lily pad with a frog on it. Explain that frogs hop from one lily pad to another to stay on top of the water but like to look in the water for bugs to eat. Explain that the student will float on her front like a lily pad and that you will place a rubber frog on her back. After you count to 3, the frog will want to look in the water for bugs, and she should stand up to allow the frog to dive or slide off her back. Remind the student to blow bubbles while lying facedown in the water and, when standing, to drive her knees forward and pull her shoulders back so the frog will dive into the water.

Student Directions

The student floats on her front and blows bubbles, making believe she is a lily pad while a rubber frog is placed on her back. After a count of 3, she stands up to allow the frog to dive off her back.

Jumping Frogs 2

Skill 2.9—Float on Front While Holding the Pool Gutter or Edge for Three Seconds While Blowing Bubbles and Recover to a Stand

Equipment

Laminated picture of a lily pad, toy frog

Preparation

Laminate a picture of a lily pad with a frog on it and have a toy frog ready.

Formation

The student faces the wall of the pool in chest- or waist-deep water, holding the gutter or edge. A laminated picture of a frog on a lily pad is taped on the edge of the pool or on a cone at the edge of the pool in front of the student. Pictures often help children conceptualize activities.

Instructor Directions

Show the student a picture of a lily pad with a frog on it. Explain that frogs hop from one lily pad to another to stay on top of the water but like to dive into the water to find bugs to eat. Tell the student that he will be pretending to be a lily pad and that you will place a toy frog on his back as soon as he is lying flat holding the gutter or pool edge with his face in the water and blowing bubbles. When you count to 3, the frog will want to dive in the water to get bugs, and the student should stand up so the frog can do that. Remind the student to blow bubbles while on his front and, when recovering to standing, to drive his knees forward and pull his shoulders back to stand up and let the frog dive into the water.

Student Directions

The student moves from standing and holding the gutter or pool edge to lying facedown on the water and blowing bubbles, pretending to be a lily pad. After you count to 3, he lifts his head, bends his knees toward his chest, pushes down on the gutter, and stands so the toy frog slide offs (or dives) into the water to retrieve bugs.

Captain's Orders 1

Skill 2.10—Float on Front Independently for Three Seconds While Blowing Bubbles and Recover to a Stand

Equipment

Pool noodle, laminated cards with commands on them (both optional)

Preparation

Think up a variety of fun positions for the student to assume, such as toy soldiers standing straight and a boat floating in the water.

Formation

The student and the instructor are standing in chest-deep water facing each other.

Instructor Directions

As the captain, give the student orders to obey. For example, if you say, "Soldier's time to sleep," the student should float on her front until you give another order. Get the student's attention before giving the next order. Another idea is to have commands on laminated index cards to show to the student. Other command examples are "Blow out candles" (the student blows bubbles) and "Attention" (the student stands on both feet at attention). This game requires prompt responses from the student.

Student Directions

The students obeys the orders given by the captain (e.g., float on the back, stand straight, float on the front, blow bubbles).

Number Fitness

Skill 2.11—Float on Front for Five Seconds Independently

Equipment

Laminated math flash cards whose sums are no more than 5 (with pictures, words, or braille)

Preparation

Laminate flash cards with math problems on them that are appropriate for the developmental level of the student. Write a floating activity on the back of each card (e.g., "float on front with one arm out to side," "float on front with legs apart").

Formation

Both the student and the instructor are in chest-deep water facing each other.

Instructor Directions

Have the student choose a flash card. On the front of the card is a math problem. On the back of the card is a floating activity. The answer to the math problem is the number of seconds the student has to perform the activity.

Student Directions

The student calculates the math problem on the flash card and performs the floating activity on the back of the card for the number of seconds that the sum of the math problem indicates.

Picture This

Skill 2.12—Float on Front for Three Seconds While Blowing Bubbles and Recover to a Stand Independently

Equipment

Five medium cones; five laminated pairs of index cards that have pictures of people in various front float positions

Preparation

Laminate five pairs of index cards (each pair is identical) that show pictures of people in various front float positions (feet together, feet apart, arms against body, arms away from body, arms and legs like the letter X). Use braille labels on the cards. Tape one of each pair of cards to a cone that is within reachable distance from the side of the pool. You should hold the other card from each pair.

Formation

The student is standing next to the instructor in chest-deep water.

Instructor Directions

Hand one of the cards to the student and instruct him to walk around the shallow end and find the matching card on a cone. When he has found it, he leaves the card under the cone, performs the float that is pictured on the card independently for three seconds, and recovers to a stand. Then he gets the next card from you and repeats until he has found all of the cards.

Student Directions

After being given a card, the student walks to find the matching card taped to a cone on the deck, puts the card under the cone on the deck, and performs the skill for three seconds independently before recovering to a stand. He then gets a new card and repeats the activity until there are no cards left.

Freeze Frame on Back

Skill 2.13—Float on Back With Instructor Support

Equipment

Floating foam mat

Preparation

Use colored tape to make a big X on the mat as a guide.

Formation

The student is facing the instructor in chest-deep water with a floating mat between them.

Instructor Directions

Demonstrate lying on the mat, and then help the student onto the mat and encourage her to lie on her back with arms and legs spread out on top of the colored X made with tape. Support her in this assisted floating position. Have her wiggle her arms and legs. When you say "Freeze frame," have her return to the X position on the mat. You can adjust her arms or legs and remind her about the proper head position. This can be practiced out of the pool first.

Student Directions

The student lies on the mat like an X or a starfish or any other formation you describe. When you say "Wiggle," she wiggles her arms and legs; when you say "Freeze frame," she returns to lying still on the mat with her arms and legs spread out like the letter X.

Things Are Looking Up

Skill 2.13—Float on Back With Instructor Support

Equipment

Pool noodle (if necessary)

Preparation

None

Formation

The instructor squats in the water at the student's level. The student is on her back (supine position) with her head resting on the instructor's shoulder.

Instructor Directions

Support the student while making up a scenario such as star gazing or looking for airplanes to help her keep her head back. If the student enjoys *The Lion King*, you can explain that you are going to reenact the scene in which Simba, Timon, and Pumbaa look up at the stars and talk about what they think stars are made of. Provide support by having the student use your shoulder as a pillow on which to relax. A noodle can be placed at the student's hips for extra help floating. Use a scenario that does not address sight for those who cannot see.

Student Directions

The student rests her head on your shoulder and floats on her back while listening to your story.

Sing Loud and Proud

Skill 2.13—Float on Back With Instructor Support

Equipment
None

Preparation
Make up a song or story about the letter X. You can use children's songs or poems and change the words.

Formation
The instructor is standing behind the student, who will be in chest-deep water.

Instructor Directions
Sing your song or recite your story about floating in the shape of an X. For example, instead of singing "The itsy bitsy spider goes up the water spout," change the words to "Billy makes an X shape and keeps his belly up."

Student Directions
The student rests his head on your shoulder and listens to the lyrics of the song or the words of the story. When you say "X," he has to make an X with his body on the water.

Head, Shoulders, Knees, and Toes

Skill 2.14—Float on Back and Recover to a Stand With Instructor's Help

Equipment
None

Preparation
None

Formation
The student and the instructor start on the deck and then move into chest-deep water facing each other.

Instructor Directions
Standing with the student on the deck, sing the song "Head, Shoulders, Knees and Toes." Make sure the student is pointing to the correct body parts. Move into the pool and have the student float on her back while you sing the song. Encourage her to bring her knees in until she is standing up at the end. The song lyrics are:

Head, shoulders, knees and toes, knees and toes

Head, shoulders, knees and toes, knees and toes

Eyes and ears and mouth and nose

Head, shoulders, knees and toes, knees and toes

Student Directions

The student sings the song with you on the pool deck and points to the various body parts mentioned in the song. Then she moves into chest-deep water with you and floats on her back while pointing to the various body parts. When she touches her nose, she recovers to a stand.

Jumping Frogs 3

Skill 2.14—Float on Back and Recover to a Stand With Instructor's Help

Equipment

Laminated picture of a frog on a lily pad, toy frog

Preparation

Laminate a picture of a lily pad with a frog on it, and have a toy frog on hand.

Formation

The student and the instructor are in chest-deep water with the instructor standing behind the student.

Instructor Directions

Show the student a picture of a frog on a lily pad. Explain that frogs hop from one lily pad to another to stay on top of the water but like to dive into the water to find bugs to eat. Explain that the student will pretend to be a lily pad (lying on his back on the water) and that you will place a toy frog on his belly button. Tell him that after a count of 3, the frog wants to dive to get bugs and that he should stand up to allow the frog to dive off his belly.

Student Directions

The student pretends to be a lily pad, lying on his back on the water with your hand under him. After you count to 3, he stands up so the frog slides off his belly and dives underwater to look for bugs.

Captain's Orders 2

Skill 2.15—Float on Back and Recover to a Stand With One Hand on the Pool Gutter or Edge

Equipment

Pool noodle (optional)

Preparation

None

Formation

The student stands next to the pool gutter or edge holding on with one hand, facing the instructor, in chest-deep water.

Instructor Directions

As the captain, give orders that the student must obey. For example, if you say, "Soldier's time to sleep," the student floats on her back, holding the gutter or pool edge until you give another order. Get the student's attention before giving the next order. Another idea is to have laminated index cards with the commands written or depicted on them. Another example of an order is "Attention" (the student has to stand on both feet at attention). This game requires prompt responses from the student.

Student Directions

The student obeys each order you call (e.g., float on the back, stand straight) until another order is called.

Hugs and Kisses

Skill 2.16—Float on Back and Recover to a Stand Independently

Equipment

None

Preparation

None

Formation

The student and the instructor are in chest-deep water facing each other and holding hands.

Instructor Directions

This game is a fun way to teach students to stand up independently while using hydrodynamics principles. Demonstrate a back float with your arms and legs out to your sides like an X (kiss), and then demonstrate an O (hug) by bringing your arms to your knees and curling up. This should cause your bottom to sink. Then demonstrate recovering to a stand by moving to the vertical position and standing up and making a vertical X.

Student Directions

The student starts off floating on top of the water as an X (horizontal), and then curls into a ball to make an O. This should cause her legs to sink and move her to a vertical position so she can stand up and make a vertical X.

In the Hugs and Kisses activity, the swimmer tucks into a ball to make the letter O to begin the recovery from the back float.

Tick Tock Time Me

Skill 2.17—Float on Back for Five Seconds Independently

Equipment
Waterproof watch with a timer

Preparation
None

Formation
The student is in chest-deep water facing the instructor.

Instructor Directions
Demonstrate the back float and ask the student to time you. Then ask the student to perform a back float and time how long he can float. Each day the student can set a new goal for a longer time.

Student Directions
When you say "Go," the student floats on his back and tries to beat his floating time from the last swim session.

One to Ten

Skill 2.17—Float on Back for Five Seconds Independently

Equipment
Laminated cards printed with the numbers 1 to 10 (optional)

Preparation
Laminate index cards bearing the numbers 1 to 10. Develop your own point system for how well the student performs a back float for five seconds. For example, you can assign points for not moving, for pointing the toes, or for gracefulness.

Formation
The student is in chest-deep water facing the instructor.

Instructor Directions
Tell the student that you are in the Floating Olympics. Demonstrate a perfect 10 float and explain what constitutes a perfect 10 float. Then have the student perform a float and hold up a card to indicate the score (as in gymnastics and diving competitions in the Olympics). A perfect 10 might be awarded for floating for five seconds independently without moving.

Student Directions
Once you say "Go," the student floats on her back, working on good form. When she is finished, she looks to see the score you awarded.

Flutter Kicking on the Back

Kicking is an important skill for propulsion and stability in swimming. The kick should originate at the hip rather than knee. In the flutter kick, the legs should stay relatively straight with a slight knee bend and move up and down in opposition so that the water looks like it is boiling near the feet. The torso typically is rolling slightly to the right and left during flutter kicking on the back (see figure L2.4).

Cues

- Have floppy ankles.
- Boil water with your toes.
- Have long legs (to promote limited knee bend).
- Power from your core and kick from your hips.

Differentiation

- If a student does not have mobility of the lower extremities or does not have one or both lower extremities, hold his trunk or allow him to use a flotation device such as a pool noodle. The ultimate goals are to encourage independence and for the student to compensate, as much as possible, with his upper body. Students can rotate their bodies from side to side to create waves.
- For those with lower-body challenges, use arm motions (e.g., like a bird) as a substitute for kicking.
- Let students with poor upper-body control lie on a floating pool mat.
- Provide tactile cues (hands on) for those who cannot see demonstrations.
- Use U.S. Coast Guard–approved PFDs or adult assistance with students who need more support.
- Have students who cannot move their lower legs create waves by moving their bodies up and down (body undulation).
- Use an object with sound localization for students with no vision to move toward.

Figure L2.4   Flutter kicking on the back, making sure that the kick originates from the hip.

Flower Showers

Skill 2.18—Flutter Kick on Back While Being Towed 12 Yards by the Instructor

Equipment
Kickboard or other floating, flat object attached to a string; plastic flowers or a plastic bowl

Preparation
Place the plastic flowers (or bowl) on a kickboard or floating object. Attach the kickboard to a string that you will hold. The string must be long enough so that when the student is floating on her back with your support, her feet do not touch the kickboard behind her.

Formation
The instructor is standing behind the student, supporting the student's back. The instructor is holding a string attached to a kickboard that is trailing about 1 foot (30 cm) behind the student's feet.

Instructor Directions
While supporting the student's back, tell her to flutter kick so that her splashes water the flowers. Another option is to place a plastic bowl on the kickboard and challenge the student to fill the bowl with water without kicking it over.

Student Directions
When you say "Go," the student flutter kicks and makes big splashes to water the flowers or fill the bowl.

Fin Fun

Skill 2.18—Flutter Kick on Back While Being Towed 12 Yards by the Instructor

Equipment
Fins, a stopwatch (optional)

Preparation
Help the student put on the fins, if necessary.

Formation
The student is wearing fins and standing next to the instructor in chest-deep water.

Instructor Directions
Provide as much support as needed to the student, who is floating on his back. Tell him to kick and keep the fins underwater. Tow the student 12 yards pointing out that fins help him point his toes and go faster. You can time the student with and without the fins. While the student is kicking, provide support by holding him by the shoulders.

Student Directions

Once you say "Go," the student begins by kicking with straight legs and toes pointed, trying to keep his feet from coming out of the water, while you hold him by the shoulders.

Tossed Salad

Skill 2.18—Flutter Kick on Back While Being Towed 12 Yards by the Instructor

Equipment

Plastic food such as lettuce, tomatoes, and cucumber slices; floating lane line divider

Preparation

Place plastic food items within a 2-foot (61 cm) radius in the shallow end. Put a floating lane line divider across the shallow end so that the objects don't drift into the deep end.

Formation

The student faces the instructor in chest-deep water; floating plastic salad items are within 2 feet (61 cm) of them.

Instructor Directions

Hold the student on her back in the middle of the food items and ask her to kick her feet to toss the salad. Tow the student around for 12 yards while she kicks her feet. Use fun terms as she is doing this, such as "Salad spinner! Go, go, go."

Student Directions

While on her back (towed by the instructor), the student kicks her feet to mix the salad items. You can use other floating plastic foods to make a cake, mix the pancake batter, and so on.

Entry and Exit Skills Without a Ladder

Entering and exiting a pool without a ladder is a fundamental safety skill for all students. It requires core and upper-body strength. When students are practicing these skills, support them so they don't hit their heads or faces on the side of the pool.

Cues

- Jump up.
- Push with your arms.
- Twist your body in the air.
- Sit on the edge of the pool.

Differentiation

- Support students with limited upper-body strength by holding them by the waist.
- Place a plastic crate at the bottom of the pool as a step, until students can perform the skill by themselves.
- Provide a mat along the side of the pool for students who may need the cushioning.

Human Rocket and Landing 1

Skill 2.19—Get out of the Water Without a Ladder With Instructor Support

Equipment
None

Preparation
None

The instructor provides support for the swimmer to be a human rocket.

Formation
The student holds the gutter or pool edge with two hands, while the instructor supports her by the trunk. The student is standing in waist- or chest-deep water.

Instructor Directions
Hold the student with one hand on each side of his trunk. Instruct him to perform five bobs and then to take off (jump up) as high as appropriate and twist to a sitting position on the edge of the pool. You can start this activity by saying, "It's time to be a human rocket!" The rocket ship must prepare five rocket boosters (bob five times) before takeoff.

Student Directions
When you say, "The rocket ship must prepare five rocket boosters before takeoff," the student bobs five times and takes off (jumps up) as high as appropriate and twists to a sitting position on the edge of the pool. After bobbing, the student may need an extra boost from you to get high enough to twist to a sitting position on the pool deck.

Before doing this activity, explain to the student that this is not a competition. Safety is extremely important at all times, especially when getting out of the pool.

Human Rocket and Landing 2

Skill 2.20—Get out of the Water Without a Ladder Independently

Equipment
None

Preparation
None

Formation
The student starts by holding on to the side of the pool with two hands. The student is standing in waist-deep or chest-deep water.

Instructor Directions
Start this activity by saying, "The rocket ship must prepare five rocket boosters before takeoff." Then say "It is time to be a human rocket!" The student bobs five times (to get momentum) and then jumps up, pushing his hands down on the pool ledge. The student takes off as high as appropriate and twists to a sitting position on the edge of the pool. Watch him closely for safety issues.

Be sure to spot the student near the pool edge so he does not hit his chin. Safety is extremely important at all times, especially when getting out of the pool.

Student Directions
The student starts by holding the side of the pool with two hands. When you say, "The rocket ship must prepare five rocket boosters before takeoff," the student bobs five times and then jumps up (takes off) as high as appropriate and twists to a sitting position on the edge of the pool.

Water Entry: Jumping

Jumping is a fun way to get in the water. A high level of safety awareness is needed when jumping feet-first from the pool deck; jumping into the water a safe distance from the wall and other people takes practice.

Cues
- Make sure the water is clear to jump into.
- Bend knees.
- Jump forward.
- Go feet-first.
- Land with bent knees.
- Blow bubbles.
- Stand up.

Differentiation

- Students who do not have the use of their lower extremities can start in a sitting position on a wet mat at the edge of the pool and slide into the pool using their hands.
- If a student lacks strength in the arms or lower body, you can support him by the trunk.

Slip Slide

Skill 2.21—Jump Into Chest-Deep Water From a Sitting Position, Holding the Instructor's Hand

Equipment
Foam mat

Preparation
Wet the surface of a foam, wrestling, or gym mat before the student slides so there is no rubbing on the skin.

Formation
The student is sitting on the pool deck in an area that is safe, low traffic, and close to a pool entry point, and facing the instructor, who is in at least chest-deep water.

Instructor Directions
Tell the student that this activity help her learn to jump into the water. Make sure the mat has water on it right before sliding so there is no uncomfortable rubbing of the legs. Use reassuring cues (e.g., "I will support you all the way down"). Hold the student's hand and guide her into the water.

Student Directions
Once you say "Go," the student sits on the mat and slides into the pool on her bottom, while holding your hand.

High Jump

Skill 2.21—Jump Into Chest-Deep Water From a Sitting Position, Holding the Instructor's Hand

Equipment
Pool noodle

Preparation
None

Formation
The student is seated on the edge of the pool; the instructor is in chest-deep water holding his hands over a floating pool noodle.

Instructor Directions

Place a pool noodle on the water in front of you so you are reaching over it to hold the student's hands. Ask the student to jump over the noodle into the water.

Student Directions

The student sits on the pool edge holding your hands. When you say "Go," the student jumps (i.e., leans forward lifting his bottom) from the sitting position over the noodle and into the water.

Slam Dunk

Skill 2.22—Jump Into Chest-Deep Water From a Standing Position, Holding the Instructor's Hand

Equipment

Pool noodle, pool noodle connector

Preparation

Bend a pool noodle and connect the ends with a noodle connector.

Formation

The student is standing on the edge of the pool, toes over the edge; the instructor is in the water, holding one of her hands. With the other hand, the instructor holds the circular noodle 3 feet (1 m) away from the wall.

Instructor Directions

Tell the student to pretend to be a basketball that wants to slam dunk into the basketball rim (circular noodle). On the command "Slam dunk," the student jumps into the hoop and with her free hand grabs the rim (noodle), just like basketball players do when they dunk the ball! To motivate the student, you can create a story in which she is in the WNBA final and you can count down to when she should jump. Once the student jumps or slides in (if she cannot jump), cheer with her to celebrate the accomplishment.

Student Directions

Once you say "Go," the student jumps from a standing position, holding one of your hands, into the circular noodle. Once she has jumped or slid in (if she cannot jump), she shouts a chant, celebrating her accomplishment.

Walk the Plank

Skill 2.22—Jump Into Chest-Deep Water From a Standing Position, Holding the Instructor's Hand

Equipment

Two dark-colored bath mats (laid end to end they should be 5 ft, or 1.5 m, long)

Preparation

Line up the mats perpendicular to the pool to make a pathway.

Formation

The instructor is in the water about 5 feet from the edge. The student is standing on the pool deck, assisted by another adult, at the beginning of the bath mat (plank). The student is in an area of the pool deck that is safe, low-traffic, and close to a pool entry point.

Instructor Directions

Start the activity by encouraging the child to walking over the plank (i.e., the bath mat that is perpendicular to the pool edge). When the student gets to the edge of the pool, grasp his hand and hel him to jump in. Remind him to bend his knees to absorb the jump when his feet hit the bottom.

Student Directions

The student walks on the bath mat (plank) toward the pool and, as he gets close to the edge, takes the instructor's extended hand and jumps into the pool.

Smile for the Camera

Skill 2.23—Jump Into Chest-Deep Water Independently

Equipment

Pool noodle, noodle connector or hula hoop

Preparation

Connect the pool noodle at the ends with the noodle connector to form a floating ring (unless using a hula hoop).

Formation

The student is standing on the edge of the pool; the instructor is in chest-deep water 5 feet from the edge.

Instructor Directions

Demonstrate a jump off the side into the hoop or circular noodle, and then ask the student to do the same. Tell the student that when she jumps, she must be smiling because you are going to take a picture with your hands (or a parent can actually take a photo from across the pool). When the student finishes her jump, she rotates the circular foam noodle to make a frame and smiles at the instructor.

Student Directions

The student stands on the edge of the pool. At your signal she jumps into the water into the hoop or circular noodle. When she jumps, she smiles as you pretend to take a picture with your hands. When the student finishes her jump, she rotates the circular foam noodle to make a frame and smiles at the instructor.

Olympic Pool Jumping

Skill 2.23—Jump Into Chest-Deep Water Independently

Equipment
Laminated index cards labeled 1 to 10 (optional)

Preparation
None

Formation
The student is standing on the edge of the pool at the chest-deep area.

Instructor Directions
Set a scenario in which the student is an Olympic jumper and you are the judge. After the student jumps in, you judge him on a scale of 1 to 10, giving appropriate marks for each jump. The categories could include largest splash, smallest splash, biggest smile, and funniest jump. Instead of just saying the number, you can hold scoring cards (just as in diving meets). When the student resurfaces, hold up or announce the score he received.

Student Directions
The student is standing on the edge of the pool. At your signal, he jumps into the water. When he resurfaces, he looks (or listens) for his score.

Deep Water Exploration

Hanging on to the gutter or the pool edge and exploring the deep end is an important task to master before swimming in the deep end. Students must be able to hold on to the wall with both hands to keep their heads above water with ease.

Cues
- Curl your fingers around the edge.
- Keep your shoulders in the water.

Differentiation
- Students with no upper-body strength or who are missing one or both extremities can use a flotation device or be supported by an assistant.

Spiderman

Skill 2.24—Hang on to the Pool Gutter or Edge in Deep Water, Submerge the Whole Body, and Recover to the Surface

Equipment
Lane lines or hoops

Preparation

Place obstacles such as lane lines and hoops along the edge of the pool for the student to negotiate while hand crawling from the shallow end to the deep end.

Formation

The student is standing next to the instructor and holding the pool gutter or edge in shallow water.

Instructor Directions

Show the student how to "spider" (i.e., slide her hands along the pool gutter or edge to move from one area to another) in the shallow end. Then ask the student to spider (hand crawl) into the deep water and submerge her whole body while holding the pool gutter or edge like Spiderman. There will be obstacles that Spiderman needs to overcome and go underwater to avoid (e.g., lane lines or hoops).

Student Directions

The student hand crawls (spiders) like Spiderman around the pool. She starts in the shallow end and then moves along the wall into the deep end, negotiating obstacles along the way.

In Spiderman, the swimmer tries to avoid obstacles while moving along the gutter.

Building on Basic Skills

Modified Texas Woman's University Aquatic Assessment: Level 3

Student's name: _____ Instructor's name: _____

Student's date of birth: _____ Date: _____

Page number	Skill number	Skill description	Yes	No	Comments
92	3.1	Bob for 10 seconds in chin-deep water			
93	3.2	Bob for 20 seconds in chin-deep water			
95	3.3	Breathe in with the ear in the water and roll the head to blow bubbles in the water five consecutive times while holding the pool gutter or edge			
96	3.4	Breathe in with the ear in the water and roll the head to blow bubbles in the water five consecutive times independently			
98	3.5	Glide on front and recover to feet with instructor's help			
99	3.6	Glide on front and recover to feet independently			
100	3.7	Glide on front fully submerged for three seconds			
103	3.8	Front crawl with arms remaining underwater (human stroke) with instructor support for 12 yards			
106	3.9	Front crawl with arms remaining underwater independently for 6 yards			
107	3.10	Front crawl with arms remaining underwater independently for 12 yards			
107	3.11	Glide on back and recover to feet with instructor support			
108	3.12	Glide on back and recover to feet independently			
109	3.13	Glide on front and then roll to back with instructor support			
110	3.14	Glide on front and then roll to back independently			

Page number	Skill number	Skill description	Yes	No	Comments
112	3.15	Glide on back and then roll to front with instructor support			
113	3.16	Glide on back and then roll to front independently			
114	3.17	Flutter kick 12 yards with a kickboard pulled by the instructor			
115	3.18	Flutter kick 6 yards with a kickboard independently			
117	3.19	Flutter kick 12 yards with a kickboard independently			
119	3.20	Jump into chin-deep water and return safely to the side			
121	3.21	Tread in chin-deep water for 10 seconds			
122	3.22	Hang on to the pool gutter or edge in at least 9 feet (2.7 m) of water, submerge the full body, and recover to the surface			
123	3.23	Hang on to the pool gutter or edge in at least 9 feet (2.7 m) of water, submerge the full body, release the gutter or edge, and kick up to the surface independently			

General comments:

Modified from Texas Woman's University Aquatic Assessment.

From M. Lepore, L. Columna, and L. Friedlander Litzner, 2015, *Assessments and activities for teaching swimming* (Champaign, IL: Human Kinetics).

Level 3 of the modified TWU aquatic assessment focuses on building the skills needed for propulsion and swim strokes and continuing to practice entering the pool by jumping. Students at level 3 need to have mastered the prerequisites in levels 1 and 2 to be safe with and successful at learning level 3 skills.

Level 3 is the level at which most students with some exposure to aquatic environments typically begin. It reviews some skills introduced in level 2, such as bobbing, but at higher levels. Additional skills at this level are rhythmic breathing and gliding, which are essential to the most basic swimming skill, the front crawl (freestyle). Level 3 comprises 23 swimming skills. Students at this level learn to combine breathing and gliding while performing the front crawl and, at the same time, progress to the integration of the flutter kick.

The more advanced skills at this level are jumping, treading water, and full body submersion. These skills are prerequisites to the safety skills and more advanced skills that are introduced in levels 4 through 6.

Don't forget that these activities represent general ideas you can use to make the aquatic experience fun. Feel free to modify any of the activities and to add some of your own.

Bobbing

In level 2, students bob in chest-deep water. In level 3, they bob in chin-deep water for a longer period of time.

Measure That 1

Skill 3.1—Bob for 10 Seconds in Chin-Deep Water

Equipment
Pool noodle with measurement markings along its length

Preparation
Make sure there is a clear area around the student in the pool. Use a noodle to create a measuring device to mark how high the student can jump (see the photo for the How High activity in level 2).

Formation
The student and the instructor are in chin-deep water facing each other.

Instructor Directions
Explain to the student that, on your signal, she is to bob in the water while you count to 10, at which point she should jump up as high as possible and touch the noodle. Use a pool noodle with a measurement device on it to see the highest jump the student can reach. On each jump (bob), the student submerges and blows bubbles.

Student Directions
The student bobs continuously for 10 seconds and then jumps as high as possible and touches the pool noodle.

10-Second Rush

Skill 3.1—Bob for 10 Seconds in Chin-Deep Water

Equipment
None

Preparation
None

Formation
The student and the instructor are in chin-deep water facing each other.

Instructor Directions

Count how many bobs the student can do in 10 seconds, touching the bottom of the pool. Each day have the student try to beat the previous day's record.

Student Directions

The student submerges underwater, touches the pool bottom, and blows bubbles; she does this as many times as possible in 10 seconds.

Bull's-Eye

Skill 3.1—Bob for 10 Seconds in Chin-Deep Water

Equipment

Pool noodle, noodle connector or hula hoop

Preparation

Use the noodle connector to make the pool noodle into a circle, unless you are using a hula hoop.

Formation

The student is in chin-deep water facing the instructor, who is holding a circular pool noodle or a hula hoop about a foot (30 cm) above the water over the student's head.

Instructor Directions

Ask the student to bob up and down while keeping himself inside the circle of the pool noodle or hula hoop (i.e., the bull's-eye). To differentiate the activity, you can hold the noodle or hula hoop higher or lower.

Student Directions

The student bobs up and down for 10 seconds within the circular noodle or hula hoop, trying to get a bull's-eye every time.

Measure That 2

Skill 3.2—Bob for 20 Seconds in Chin-Deep Water

Equipment

Pool noodle with measurement markings along its length

Preparation

Make sure there is a clear area around the student in the pool. Create a measuring device with a noodle to mark how high the student can jump.

Formation

The student and the instructor are in chin-deep water facing each other.

Instructor Directions

Demonstrate bobbing, and then tell the student to bob for 20 seconds. When 20 seconds is completed, say "Measure that," which is the signal for the student to jump as high as possible and touch the pool noodle.

Student Directions

The student bobs continuously for 20 seconds and then jumps as high as possible and touches the pool noodle to determine how high she jumped.

20-Second Rush

Skill 3.2—Bob for 20 Seconds in Chin-Deep Water

Equipment
None

Preparation
None

Formation
The student and the instructor are in chin-deep water facing each other.

Instructor Directions
Count how many bobs the student can do in 20 seconds, touching the bottom of the pool. Each day have the student try to beat the previous day's record.

Student Directions
The student tries to do as many bobs as possible in 20 seconds, touching the bottom of the pool. The student must submerge underwater and blow bubbles during each bob.

Breath Control

Figure L3.1   Students at this level can practice rhythmic breathing to the side.

Breath control during aquatic activities is unique: students must breathe in when their mouths are out of the water and out when they are in the water (see figure L3.1). Because all swim strokes and most aquatic activities involve breath control, it is a very important skill to practice.

Cues for Breath Control: Rhythmic Breathing to the Side
- Ear in water, breathe in.
- Point nose to the pool bottom; blow bubbles.
- Repeat.

Differentiation
- Allow students to use a mask while learning the skill.
- Use a flotation device under the chest during breath control practice.

Bubble Straw

Skill 3.3—Breathe in With the Ear in the Water and Roll the Head to Blow Bubbles in the Water Five Consecutive Times While Holding the Pool Gutter or Edge

Equipment
Drinking straws

Preparation
Have a straw ready for both you and the student.

Formation
The student is in waist-deep water holding the pool edge or gutter.

Instructor Directions
Using a straw, demonstrate how to breathe in and then how to blow bubbles in the water. Also demonstrate how to turn the head to the side and breathe in with the straw and then put your face in the water and blow bubbles using the straw.

Student Directions
The student blows bubbles in the water with a straw and, keeping the head facing down, turns his head to the side and breathes through the straw. He then repeats this sequence.

Picture Perfect

Skill 3.3—Breathe in With the Ear in the Water and Roll the Head to Blow Bubbles in the Water Five Consecutive Times While Holding the Pool Gutter or Edge

Equipment
Two laminated pictures of a mouth (brailled with a description if necessary), goggles for the student

Preparation
This activity helps the student practice when to breathe in and when to breathe out while swimming. Two pictures are needed: one with a mouth open and the words *Breathe in* and one with lips pursed and the words *Blow out*. Have the first picture in your hand and place the second on the pool bottom beneath the student.

Formation
With goggles on, the student is in waist- or chest-deep water facing the instructor.

Instructor Directions
Hold the picture of the open mouth at the water level to the side of the student (where she will be turning her head first), and place the picture of the pursed lips on the pool floor directly under the student's face.

Student Directions
With goggles on, the student rolls her head to the side with her ear to the water and looks at the picture of the open mouth. She then breathes in (as the picture directs).

Then, she turns her face into the water to look at the picture at the bottom of the pool (of the pursed lips) and blows bubbles five consecutive times.

Tick Tock Five

Skill 3.4—Breathe in With the Ear in the Water and Roll the Head to Blow Bubbles in the Water Five Consecutive Times Independently

Equipment
None

Preparation
None

Formation
The student is facing the instructor in chest-deep water.

Instructor Directions
Demonstrate rhythmic breathing to the side with a rhythm of *tick-tock, tick-tock*. When you say "Tick," the student rotates his face into the water. Two seconds later, say "Tock," which is the signal for the student to rotate his face out of the water to one side. Repeat the tick-tock command five times.

Student Directions
The student begins with one ear in the water and his face to the side. When you say "Tick," he takes a breath and rotates his head to the facedown position and blows bubbles. When you say "Tock," he rotates his head to the side to the start position and takes a breath in.

Shout Out

Skill 3.4—Breathe in With the Ear in the Water and Roll the Head to Blow Bubbles in the Water Five Consecutive Times Independently

Equipment
None

Preparation
None

Formation
The instructor and student face each other in chest-deep water.

Instructor Directions
Tell the student a word and then demonstrate how to say that word with your face in the water. (Turn your head and take a breath, return your face to the water, and say the word again.) Do this five times. Use fun words such as a favorite ice cream flavor or a favorite color.

Student Directions

The student performs rhythmic breathing, placing her ear in the water during the inhalation and saying the word you have chosen each time she puts her face in the water five consecutive times.

Gliding

Gliding involves being in a streamlined position following a kick or push off the wall and holding that position while moving forward without arm or leg motion (see figure L3.2). In general, gliding is how to start any swimming stroke from the wall, and a streamlined position is necessary to maximize efficiency.

Cues

- Squeeze your ears with your arms.
- Face in, blowing bubbles.
- Keep legs tight together.
- Look like a pencil (or ruler).

Differentiation

- Give physical assistance to a student who is not able to maintain a streamlined position.
- Use tactile modeling for those who cannot see the demonstrations.
- Use flotation devices to help students maintain a horizontal position.

Figure L3.2   Gliding is a good progression before starting any swimming stroke.

Glide Contest

Skill 3.5—Glide on Front and Recover to Feet With Instructor's Help

Equipment
None

Preparation
Make sure the area is clear of people and equipment.

Formation
The student starts in waist- or chest-deep water with her back to the wall and facing the instructor. Her hands are stretched outward as she waits for the instructor to grasp them.

Instructor Directions
While holding the student's hands, give her a verbal cue to glide. After about three seconds of gliding, tell her to stand up. If needed, you can stand to her side and guide her knees forward during the transition to the standing position. The goal of the activity is to see how far the student can go by pushing off the wall without moving her arms or legs after the push-off.

Student Directions
The student is pulled as she glides in a streamlined position off the wall. She begins with her back to the wall and then bends one knee to place one foot against the wall. Holding your hands, she puts her face in the water and blows bubbles while pushing off the wall and gliding. She does this for as long as she can hold her breath or until you say "Stand," at which point she recovers to a standing position.

Superman/Superwoman

Skill 3.5—Glide on Front and Recover to Feet With Instructor's Help

Equipment
Laminated Superman-style letter S

Preparation
Create a fun story about Superman or Superwoman. Laminate a Superman-style letter S.

Formation
The student starts in waist- or chest-deep water with his back to the wall facing the instructor and holding the laminated Superman S with both hands.

Instructor Directions
Demonstrate the front glide and then assist the student by holding his hands (which are holding the Superman S), and give the command to glide. After three seconds, or however long you choose, give the command to stand.

Student Directions

The student holds the Superman S and puts one foot on the wall. With his face in the water, he pushes off the wall like Superman, holding the letter S in front of him. He recovers to a standing position when you give the command to stand.

Superman to Frankenstein

Skill 3.6—Glide on Front and Recover to Feet Independently

Equipment

Hand padcles (if available)

Preparation

Before starting this activity, explain that Superman flies with his hands straight over his head, and Frankenstein walks with his arms straight out in front of him.

Formation

The student is standing in the waist- or chest-deep water with her back to the wall and facing the instructor.

Instructor Directions

Explain to the student that to stand up in the water, she needs to remember the way Superman and Frankenstein hold their arms. Demonstrate the two versions.

Student Directions

Following your commands, the student glides on her front with her arms above her head like Superman. To stand up, she pushes the water toward the bottom of the pool and moves her arms so they look like Frankenstein's. For extra help, the student should bring her knees closer to her body while standing.

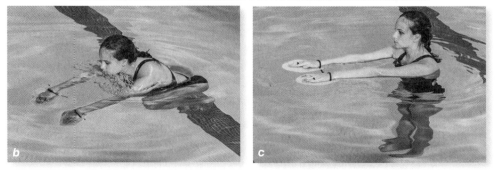

The student performs *(a)* Superman and *(b)* Frankenstein in order to *(c)* stand up in the water. Paddles may assist with this activity, but the activity can be performed without them as well.

Count It, Glide It

Skill 3.6—Glide on Front and Recover to Feet Independently

Equipment
Pool noodle cut into three pieces

Preparation
Cut a pool noodle into three pieces about 6 inches (15 cm) long. Write a number on each piece in permanent ink. Float these pieces about 4 feet (1.2 m) from the student.

Formation
The student is in waist- or chest-deep water with his back to the wall with one foot on the wall in preparation to push off into a front glide.

Instructor Directions
Demonstrate performing a front glide from the wall, grabbing a noodle piece, and walking with it back to the wall. Then ask the student to do the same. Once he has retrieved all three pieces, he adds the numbers on them and performs that many glides. Move the noodle pieces closer to or farther from the student depending on his success.

Student Directions
The student performs a front glide to grab a noodle piece. He then recovers to a stand independently, walks back to the wall with the noodle piece, puts it on the deck, and repeats. After he has retrieved all three pieces, he adds the numbers and performs that many glides.

Hole in One

Skill 3.7—Glide on Front Fully Submerged for Three Seconds

Equipment
Three to six hula hoops of different colors, brightly colored nylon rope, diving bricks (one for each hula hoop)

Preparation
Attach one end of a 6-inch (15 cm) brightly colored nylon rope to a diving brick and the other end to a hula hoop. Do this for all of the hoops and then submerge them in the water approximately 5 feet (1.5 m) from the wall in chest-deep water (they should be completely submerged).

Formation
The student is against the wall in chest-deep water with one foot against the wall.

Instructor Directions
Demonstrate gliding off the wall fully submerged in a streamlined position, passing through a hula hoop, and recovering to a stand. Explain that when you call out

The swimmer makes a hole in one when she swims through the hoop and reaches the other side.

a color, the student is to glide through a hoop of that color and then stand up to receive a high five.

Student Directions

The student glides through a hula hoop of the color you called and gets a high five after she has recovered to a stand. She then jogs back to the wall and waits for you to call another color.

Color Memory

Skill 3.7—Glide on Front Fully Submerged for Three Seconds

Equipment

Three to six hula hoops of different colors, brightly colored nylon rope, diving bricks (one for each hula hoop)

Preparation

Attach 6-inch (15 cm) lengths of brightly colored nylon rope from each diving brick to each hula hoop. Submerge the hula hoops in the water approximately 5 feet (1.5 cm) from the wall in chest-deep water (they should be completely submerged).

Formation

The student is against the wall in chest-deep water with one foot against the wall.

Instructor Directions

Explain that you will be calling out a sequence of two colors. The student's task is to push off the wall to glide through the first hoop in the sequence and then push off the bottom of the pool to glide to the second hoop while remaining fully submerged and in the streamlined position.

Student Directions

The student must remember the sequence of colors and then glide on her front in a streamlined position through the hoops in that sequence; she must remain fully submerged until she completes the sequence. When she is finished, she returns to the wall to hear another sequence.

Front Crawl

The front crawl is performed in a prone position, with the face in the water and the body about horizontal (see figure L3.3); the student performs rhythmic breathing to the side. The arms move forward in opposition while the student gently rolls the body and continuously kicks using the flutter kick. When breathing, the student should rotate her head to the side (not forward) of the arm that is out of the water. A variation of the front crawl is the human stroke, in which the arms are not brought all the way out of the water and the breathing is to the front or side. The swimmer typically begins in a doggie paddle, gradually bringing the elbow out of the water and then eventually the hand, where it progresses into the front crawl. Some people call the front crawl the freestyle stroke because swimmers sometimes choose it during freestyle competitive events because for many it is the fastest stroke.

Cues

- Keep your body horizontal.
- Breathe to the side.
- Keep your elbows high.
- Roll your body.
- Reach forward.
- Pull back toward your pocket.
- Kick to boil water.

Figure L3.3   In the front crawl, *(a)* the flutter kick is continuous as the swimmer breathes while turning his head to the side. *(b)* With his face in the water, the swimmer does the arm recovery with elbows high.

Differentiation

- Students who need extra help may use water jog belts, pool noodles under their hips, fins to help with kicking, verbal cues, or physical assistance.
- Use braille or large print on visual information and auditory sounds for targets, if necessary.
- Substitute arm motions for leg motions, if necessary, and vice versa.
- Use sign language or hand gestures for those who are deaf or hard of hearing.
- Post laminated written description of activities.

Beach Ball Soccer

Skill 3.8—Front Crawl With Arms Remaining Underwater (Human Stroke) With Instructor Support for 12 Yards

Equipment
Tape or cones to mark a goal, beach ball

Preparation
Blow up a beach ball, and place two floating markers 12 yards in front of the student.

Formation
The student and the instructor are in chest-deep water next to each other.

Instructor Directions
Demonstrate how to move the arms in opposition to push a beach ball into the goal that is 12 yards away. If needed, provide support under the belly or at the hips.

Student Directions
The student tries to move a beach ball 12 yards by extending her arms all the way out in front of her and poking the ball along the water surface. She must remain horizontal with her face up and flutter kicking.

Zip It Up

Skill 3.8—Front Crawl With Arms Remaining Underwater (Human Stroke) With Instructor Support for 12 Yards

Equipment
None

Preparation
None

Formation
The student is in chest-deep water with her back to the wall, facing an area that is at least 12 yards long. The instructor is standing near the student to offer support as needed.

The front crawl uses a motion similar to closing up your sides with a zipper. Here the swimmer has progressed to getting her elbow out of the water on the recovery. She is on her way to progressing from the human stroke to a mature front crawl.

Instructor Directions

Perform a demonstration of the front crawl, exaggerating the arm movement like you are reaching out to grab the pull of a zipper with one hand, pulling that zipper down your midline toward your thigh, and then lifting your elbow and zipping it back up your side (one arm at a time), using your thumb. Tell the student to pretend there is a zipper on each side of her trunk and that she is to pretend to grab the zipper pull from in front of her and, one arm at a time, push the zipper down her side toward her hip. When she can, encourage her to begin bringing her elbow out of the water, making progress toward a mature front crawl. Help her as needed, and provide feedback when necessary.

Student Directions

The student pushes off the wall on her front, accepting assistance as needed, and pretends to grab a zipper pull and zip down at the midline of her body toward her thighs, and then pull it back up her side (one arm at a time), using her thumb. Every time she reaches out with her hand, her thumb must graze from her hip to her armpit, forming a fin with the bent elbow, and vice versa. She continues the stroke, alternating sides. The student may begin to learn this with her arms recovering underwater and then make progress toward the elbow coming out of the water, and eventually the hand out of the water as well.

The Riddler

Skill 3.8—Front Crawl With Arms Remaining Underwater (Human Stroke) With Instructor Support for 12 Yards

Equipment

Kickboard, personalized laminated index clue cards with riddles on them related to aquatics

Preparation

Place the laminated clue cards to the edge of the pool around a 12-yard designated area.

Formation

The student is in the water lying prone on a kickboard; the instructor is by her side providing only the amount of assistance she needs to stay on the kickboard.

Instructor Directions

Demonstrate how to do the human stroke while lying on a kickboard; then explain the riddle game and provide the first laminated clue card. After the student listens or reads the clue card, hold her while she performs the human stroke while balanced on the kickboard. Guide the student to the next card until she finishes all the cards and has human stroked at least 12 yards. Riddles should be positioned all over the pool (either floating on other kickboards or taped to the side of the pool). Here is an example of a three-part riddle: *Card 1:* I can float. *Card 2:* I am not soft. *Card 3:* You can hold onto me with your hands. *Answer:* the kickboard.

Student Directions

The student performs the human stroke on a kickboard, going from clue card to clue card, and answers the riddles while the instructor holds her waist.

Scoop the Ice Cream

Skill 3.8—Front Crawl With Arms Remaining Underwater (Human Stroke) With Instructor Support for 12 Yards

Equipment

Ice cream scoopers or a cesta (the basket used to catch and throw the ball in the game of jai alai), slotted serving spoons

Preparation

Before this activity, ask the student what his favorite type of ice cream is and explain that he is going to search for some of that type of ice cream.

Formation

The student is standing in the water with his back to the pool wall.

Instructor Directions

Let the student experiment with the slotted serving spoon and the ice cream scooper and show how the ice cream scoop transfers more water. Then point out that the student's hand is like an ice cream scooper when his fingers are together and like a slotted spoon when his fingers are apart. Hold his hips and have him pretend that his hands are scoops, scooping his favorite ice cream, for 6 yards. Then have him do the same back to the starting spot.

Student Directions

The student experiments with an ice cream scooper and slotted spoon to see which one holds more water. Then he experiments with scooping his hands with closed and open fingers. Finally, he pushes off the wall and swims 6 yards, turns around, and swims 6 yards back to the edge of the pool while keeping his hands in a scoop formation.

Zoom Zoom

Skill 3.9—Front Crawl With Arms Remaining Underwater Independently for 6 Yards

Equipment
Fins for the instructor and the student

Preparation
Put on your fins and help the student put on hers, if necessary.

Formation
The student is wearing fins and standing in chest-deep water with her back against the pool wall. The instructor is beside her, also wearing fins.

Instructor Directions
Demonstrate how to do the front crawl with fins; your arms should remain underwater as in the human stroke. Then stand 6 yards from the student and motivate her by saying "Zoom zoom" until she gets to you. Have her do this several times. This activity will help her coordinate the movement of her arms and feet.

Student Directions
Wearing fins, the student performs the front crawl with underwater arm recovery and rhythmic breathing. She swims several 6-yard segments while you say "Zoom zoom."

Word Find

Skill 3.9—Front Crawl With Arms Remaining Underwater Independently for 6 Yards

Equipment
Whiteboard or laminated paper with dry erase markers and paper towel to wipe it off, kickboard

Preparation
This activity is a variation of the traditional game of hangman. Draw blank lines on a whiteboard and set it on a kickboard 6 yards from the wall of the pool.

Formation
The student and the instructor are standing in waist- or chest-deep water by the pool wall.

Instructor Directions
Demonstrate swimming 6 yards doing the front crawl, with underwater arm recovery, from the wall to a kickboard that has a whiteboard on it. Explain that every time the student gets to the whiteboard, he may guess a letter of the hangman puzzle. Write down the letter the student guesses on the whiteboard after each 6-yard swim until the puzzle is solved.

Student Directions

Every time the student completes a 6-yard independent swim using the front crawl with his face in the water and using rhythmic breathing, he guesses a letter that might be in the word. He continues swimming until the word is completed (example: S W I M).

Sticker Fun

Skill 3.10—Front Crawl With Arms Remaining Underwater Independently for 12 Yards

Equipment

Plastic or vinyl (waterproof) stickers, laminated paper to place stickers on (sticker board)

Preparation

Laminate a piece of paper with a background that is motivating to the student (e.g., Star Wars, Candy Land, Angry Birds) and acquire a few plastic vinyl stickers.

Formation

The student is in chest-deep water with her back to the wall. The instructor is 12 yards away with a laminated sticker board and stickers.

Instructor Directions

Ask the student to perform the front crawl or human stroke without any assistance for 12 yards. If the skill is done correctly, let her choose a sticker and place it on the board.

Student Directions

The student swims her best front crawl or human stroke with her face in the water and doing rhythmic breathing for 12 yards. If she performs correctly, she then chooses a sticker and places it on the sticker board. In every session, the student can count how many stickers she has earned and try to beat her record from the previous session.

Gliding on Back

In skills 3.5 and 3.6, students were required to glide on their front and recover to their feet with your support and independently. In the following skills, students continue to develop the glide (front and back), but combine it with rolling over and being more independent performing this skill.

Back Glider

Skill 3.11—Glide on Back and Recover to Feet With Instructor Support

Equipment

None

Preparation

None

Formation

The student is in waist- or chest-deep water facing and holding the pool wall, and the instructor is behind him.

Instructor Directions

Demonstrate and explain a back glide with recovery. Tell the student to pretend he is an airplane glider. Then give the start signal and assist the student in gliding on his back and recovering to his feet.

Student Directions

The student starts by facing the pool wall and pretending he is an airplane glider. When the instructor says "Go," the student glides on his back with support. When he begins to slow down, he bends his knees (toward his chest), leans his whole body forward, and stands up.

Blast Off

Skill 3.12—Glide on Back and Recover to Feet Independently

Equipment

None

Preparation

None

Formation

The student is in waist- or chest-deep water, facing and holding the wall, with the back of her head in the water and face looking up to the sky, with her feet against the wall (ready to blast off). The instructor stands about 10 feet (3 m) away.

Instructor Directions

Explain and demonstrate the back glide blast off with independent recovery to a stand; then stand about 10 feet (3 m) from the student and act as the marker, or end point of the glide. Say "3-2-1 blastoff" to signal the student to begin the glide.

Student Directions

The student starts in waist- or chest-deep water, facing and holding the wall, with the back of her head in the water and face looking up to the sky, and with her feet against the wall (ready to blast off). On the signal "3-2-1 blastoff," she pushes off the wall on her back, face above water and arms overhead or at her side, and, in a streamlined position, tries to reach you without kicking or moving her arms. Once she slows down, she must stand up. She should try to go farther each time by using more leg power during the blastoff.

Gliding Hoop

Skill 3.12—Glide on Back and Recover to Feet Independently

Equipment
Hula hoop

Preparation
Create a fun story about why the student cannot touch the hula hoop (e.g., she is swimming through a school of fish and the only way for the slimy fish not to touch her is to glide through the hoop without touching it).

Formation
The student is in waist- or chest-deep water facing and holding the pool wall with the back of her head in the water and face looking up to the sky, with her feet placed against the wall. The instructor is in the water about 5 feet (1.5 m) from the wall holding a hula hoop vertically half in and half out of the water.

Instructor Directions
Explain that the hula hoop is a protective tunnel that will keep the student safe from the slimy fish all around her. Explain the back glide through the hoop without touching it. Once she has glided through the hoop, she is to recover to standing.

Student Directions
The student pushes off the wall into a back glide in a streamlined position, and glides through the hoop. Once she is through, she stands up, making sure her feet do not touch the hoop.

The swimmer practices the back glide in streamline position during the Gliding Hoop activity.

Save the Land Animals

Skill 3.13—Glide on Front and Then Roll to Back With Instructor Support

Equipment
Plastic land animals that float

Preparation
Float plastic land animals in the water a few feet (a meter or so) from the wall.

Formation
The student is in waist- or chest-deep water with her back against the wall and one foot against the wall.

Instructor Directions

Demonstrate front gliding off the wall toward the floating land animals, grabbing one and rolling onto your back. Explain that the land animal must be saved from the water; place it on your abdomen for two seconds before standing up. Say "Save the land animals from the water!" as a signal for the student to begin.

Student Directions

The student pushes off the wall and glides with hands forward on her front, grabs a land animal, and then turns onto her back and put the animal on her abdomen to rescue it. Finally, she recovers to a stand, brings the animal to the wall, and repeats the task until all the land animals have been saved.

1, 2, 3, Roll on Front With Me

Skill 3.13—Glide on Front and Then Roll to Back With Instructor Support

Equipment

None

Preparation

None

Formation

The student is in waist- or chest-deep water standing with his back against the wall, one foot on the wall, and his hands out in front.

Instructor Directions

Explain and demonstrate front gliding off the wall and rolling onto your back. Then stand next to the student and say "Go." As the student glides, provide physical support (as needed) and say loudly, "1, 2, 3, roll with me."

Student Directions

The student glides on his front. When he hears you say "roll with me," he rolls onto his back, counts to 3 out loud, and recovers to standing.

Gliding Golf

Skill 3.14—Glide on Front and Then Roll to Back Independently

Equipment

Hula hoop

Preparation

None

Formation

The student is in chest-deep water with her back to the wall and one foot on the wall. The instructor is in the water 5 feet away holding a hula hoop half in and half out of the water.

Instructor Directions

Explain that this is a scoring game: the number of seconds it takes to glide through the hoop and roll onto her back is the student's score. As in golf, the student wants to get a low score and try to achieve a hole in one. You can move the hoop closer or farther depending on how challenged the student wants to be. A smaller hoop or larger hoop can increase and decrease the difficulty level as well. Explain that after the student has glided through the hoop, she must roll over onto her back and float.

Student Directions

The student front glides through the hula hoop and then rolls onto her back without putting her feet down and floats. The number of seconds it takes to achieve the back float position is her score.

Flip That Pancake

Skill 3.14—Glide on Front and Then Roll to Back Independently

Equipment

None

Preparation

Create a fun story about cooking a pancake breakfast.

Formation

The student is standing in chest-deep water with his back to the wall and one foot on the wall; his hands are extended in front of him. The instructor is beside him.

Instructor Directions

Demonstrate how to glide off the wall on your front and then roll onto your back. Explain that rolling over is like being a pancake being flipped.

Student Directions

The student pushes off from the wall in a front glide and pretends he is a pancake being cooked. When he rolls onto his back, he is being flipped in a pan.

Captain's Orders 3

Skill 3.14—Glide on Front and Then Roll to Back Independently

Equipment

Pool noodle (optional)

Preparation

Come up with terms that relate to positions the student will assume during the activity.

Formation

The student is standing in chest-deep water facing the instructor.

Instructor Directions

As the captain, give commands to the student that she must obey. If she cannot hear the commands (e.g., she is underwater or splashing), touch her with a pool noodle to get her attention. Following are some suggestions for commands:

- Port: Push off the wall and roll onto your back toward the left (changing direction, not the stroke).
- Starboard: Push off the wall and roll onto your back toward the right (changing direction, not the stroke).
- Stern (back): Glide on your back.
- Bow (front): Glide on your front.
- Shark: Hold on to the side (edge) of the pool with your legs curled up to your chest.
- Pirates: Glide on your front and roll onto your back.
- Jellyfish: Float on your front.

Student Directions

The student obeys your nautical commands.

Save the Sea Animals

Skill 3.15—Glide on Back and Then Roll to Front With Instructor Support

Equipment

Plastic sea animals that sink

Preparation

Place plastic sea animals on the pool deck near the student, who is in the water.

Formation

The student is in waist- or chest-deep water facing and holding the pool edge with his knees bent and his feet on the wall, floating on his back, with a plastic sea animal on his abdomen.

Instructor Directions

Demonstrate the back glide with a plastic sea animal on your abdomen, and then roll over to drop the animal into the water. Support the student when he is rolling over to his front to drop the animal.

Student Directions

The student glides on his back from the wall with a plastic sea animal on his abdomen. With your support, he rolls to his front to rescue the sea animal by dropping it back into its natural habitat. The student then recovers to a stand, walks back to the wall, and repeats the sequence until no more sea animals are stranded on the pool deck.

1, 2, 3, Roll on Back With Me

Skill 3.15—Glide on Back and Then Roll to Front With Instructor Support

Equipment
None

Preparation
None

Formation
The student is standing in waist- or chest-deep water facing the pool wall and holding the pool edge with his feet on the wall. The instructor is standing next to the student.

Instructor Directions
Explain and demonstrate back gliding off the wall and then rolling onto your front. Then stand next to the student and say "Go." As the student glides, provide physical support (as needed) and say loudly, "1, 2, 3, roll with me."

Student Directions
The student glides on his back. When he hears you say "roll with me," he turns onto his front, counts to 3 out loud, and recovers to standing, using your assistance as needed.

Gliding Golf—Remix

Skill 3.16—Glide on Back and Then Roll to Front Independently

Equipment
Hula hoop

Preparation
None

Formation
The student is standing in chest-deep water facing and holding the wall. The instructor is holding a hula hoop half in the water, half out of the water about 5 feet (1.5 m) from the wall.

Instructor Directions
Explain that the student is to push off the wall and glide through the hula hoop on her back. Explain that the number of seconds it takes to flip over once she is through the hoop is her golf score. If she can do it in one second, she gets a hole in one. You can move the hoop closer or farther depending on how challenged the student wants to be. A smaller hoop or larger hoop can increase and decrease the difficulty level as well. Hitting the hula hoop results in a one-second penalty to the score.

Student Directions

The student back glides through the hula hoop you are holding. Once she has passed through the hoop, she must roll onto her front and float for one to three seconds.

Flutter Kick

In level 2, students performed the flutter kicks on the front and back while being towed by the instructor. In level 3, students use a flutter kick with a kickboard independently.

Motorboat Shapes

Skill 3.17—Flutter Kick 12 Yards With a Kickboard Pulled by the Instructor

Equipment

Five laminated index cards per student, cut into various shapes such as circle, square, triangle; one kickboard per student

Preparation

Cut index cards in a variety of shapes, such as circles squares, or triangles, and laminate them. Place them on the edge of the pool deck 6 yards from the starting point.

Formation

The student is in the shallow end of the pool 6 yards from the index cards and holding a kickboard, with the instructor in the water holding the front of the kickboard.

Instructor Directions

Explain and demonstrate how to use the kickboard and front flutter kick to form (trace) shapes around the shallow end. Then pull the student's kickboard while he is kicking to the index cards 6 yards away. The student chooses a shape and then (with assistance) propels himself by kicking to trace the shape on the card in the water. The activity ends when all the shapes are completed.

Student Directions

The student flutter kicks on his front, using a kickboard and your assistance as needed, to a pile of laminated shapes 6 yards away. He picks a card, identifies the shape, and then uses the kickboard to trace the shape by kicking while you help guide him through the water. Once the shape is formed, he should kick back to where he started. At that point, another student can take a turn, or the same student can begin the activity again with a new card. The activity ends when all the shape cards have been played.

Healthy Grocery Shopping

Skill 3.17—Flutter Kick 12 Yards With a Kickboard Pulled by the Instructor

Equipment

Plastic toy foods that float (some healthy and some not), kickboard

Preparation

Place several plastic toy foods in the middle of the shallow end of the pool about 6 yards from the student.

Formation

The student is in chest-deep water holding a kickboard 6 yards from the floating toy foods, with the instructor beside her.

Instructor Directions

Explain and demonstrate front flutter kicking and holding the kickboard correctly. Help the student by pulling the kickboard in one direction for 6 yards to the toy foods and encourage her to select a healthy meal by choosing foods to put on the kickboard and bringing them back to home at the starting point.

Student Directions

The student holds on to the kickboard (she can pretend it's a shopping cart or serving platter) and front flutter kicks to the food to choose a healthy meal to bring back and serve to you.

Pac-Man/Pac-Woman

Skill 3.18—Flutter Kick 6 Yards With a Kickboard Independently

Equipment

Two hula hoops, laminated picture of a Pac-Man ghost, laminated picture of a piece of fruit (e.g., a cherry), kickboard

Preparation

Make up a scenario in which the student is Pac-Man and must get away from the ghost (picture) that is directly behind him on the wall 6 yards apart. He must kick through the hoops so as not to be eaten by the ghost, and then kick back to the wall where the picture of the cherry is to redeem that fruit prize.

Formation

The student is in chest-deep water holding the kickboard with his back to the wall and one foot on the wall. The instructor is in the water about 6 yards away holding a hula hoop in each hand, half in and half out of the water.

Instructor Directions

Choose how far away to hold the hoops that the student must kick through (ideally, 6 yards away). Have the student kick away from the Pac-Man ghost, flutter kick through the first hoop, and then go around you and back through the second hoop to return to the wall for the cherry prize.

Student Directions

The student flutter kicks through one hoop 6 yards away, turns to kick through a second hoop, and then returns to the wall to retrieve the cherry prize.

Scrambled Words

Skill 3.18—Flutter Kick 6 Yards With a Kickboard Independently

Equipment

Floating objects (e.g., cut-up pool noodles) with large letters printed on them (and brailled, if necessary), kickboard

Preparation

Write the letters A through Z on the floating objects and place them 6 yards from the wall, floating in chest-deep water. You may wish to have several simple words in mind to say to the students, or you can prepare word cards that you can laminate and prop up along the edge of the pool for students to reference.

Formation

The student stands in chest-deep water holding a kickboard.

Integration of literacy into pool games makes learning more interesting.

Instructor Directions

Explain and demonstrate kicking to an object and bringing it back to the start. Tell the student that together you will make words using the letters on the retrieved objects. You can also choose a word to tell students, or prop a word card up with a small cone on the side of the pool, and direct the student to retrieve the letters needed to spell it.

Student Directions

The student flutter kicks independently on a kickboard 6 yards to retrieve one letter at a time and bring it back to the wall to make a word with your help.

Intermediate Red Light, Green Light

Skill 3.18—Flutter Kick 6 Yards With a Kickboard Independently

Equipment

Three hula hoops (red, yellow, and green), kickboard

Preparation

Have the three hula hoops by the instructor's side.

Formation

The student is standing in chest-deep water holding a kickboard out in front and facing the instructor who is standing 6 yards away.

Instructor Directions

Explain that red means stop, yellow means slow flutter kicking (small splashes), and green means fast flutter kicking. Then hold a hula hoop halfway in the water and say its color (e.g., "Yellow light" to signal the student to kick slowly); the student performs the movement through the hoop (for yellow and green) or stops if you say "Red light." You can use verbal cues or traffic light pictures.

Student Directions

The student holds the kickboard and front flutter kicks at the pace determined by the color you call (or stops if you call "Red light"). The student performs the movement through the hoop.

Are You Up for a Challenge?

Skill 3.19—Flutter Kick 12 Yards With a Kickboard Independently

Equipment

Kickboard

Preparation

None

Formation

The student is standing in chest-deep water holding a kickboard and facing the instructor, who is 12 yards away.

Instructor Directions

Provide the student with a variety of challenges for the 12-yard kick across the pool (e.g., big splashes, little splashes, smiling big, not bending the knees too much).

Student Directions

The student holds a kickboard and front flutter kicks for 12 yards according to the challenge you call out (e.g., large splashes, no splashes).

Crossroads

Skill 3.19—Flutter Kick 12 Yards With a Kickboard Independently

Equipment

Objects that students will be motivated to transport from one area to another, kickboards (one for each student)

Preparation

This team activity is appropriate for two students or more. Place an equal number of objects on both sides of the pool. Each student or team starts on opposite sides of a 12-yard area.

Formation

The students stand in chest-deep water holding kickboards.

Instructor Directions

Explain and demonstrate the front flutter kick. Then explain that when you give the command "Cross," they are to kick to the opposite end of the pool, grab one object, and return it to their home base. When you say "Roads," they must stop.

Student Directions

When you say "Cross," the students perform the front flutter kick 12 yards to the objects on the other side of the pool, grab one object, and kick back to their home base to deposit the object. Students repeat this task until you say "Roads," at which time the objects are counted to determine how many points each team earned (1 point for each object).

Spell It

Skill 3.19—Flutter Kick 12 Yards With a Kickboard Independently

Equipment

Laminated index cards of 10 short words and all the letters that make up those words, cone, two

Preparation

Write a word in large print on an index card and laminate it. Tape that word to a large cone on the pool deck on the same side of the pool as the swimmer will start. Then write each of the letters that make up the word on individual cards and laminate those. Tape the laminated letters to the pool wall 6 yards away, or on small cones placed on the deck at a reachable distance to the student. The letters can be scrambled or in order of the word on the cone.

Formation

The student stands in waist- or chest-deep water holding a kickboard, and is 6 yards from the wall where the letters are posted. The cone is on the deck (near where the student begins the activity) with a full word taped on it. The instructor stands next to or close to the student.

Instructor Directions

Demonstrate a front flutter kick with kickboard for 6 yards and how to retrieve the letters of the word that is on the cone at the start. Ask the student to read the word, or identify the letters, or say the word and have her say it back. Tell the student to perform the flutter kick to get each letter of the word, one at a time, and assemble them on her kickboard to match the word on the cone.

Student Directions

The student kicks back and forth at 6 yard intervals, collecting letters one at a time to recreate the word that they see on the cone by placing the letters on their kickboard.

Jumping

Jumping into the pool and recovering safely is a skill that involves balance, core and leg strength, and overall body coordination. A feet-first entry into the water is typically fun for children to perform. Safe instruction of this skill requires an adult in the water and one on deck to act as a spotter so that the student goes feet-first into the water a safe distance from the wall and other people. In level 2, students jump from the edge of the pool into chest-deep water mainly assisted by the instructor. In level 3, students jump into chin-deep water and return to the edge of the pool independently.

Smile

Skill 3.20—Jump Into Chin-Deep Water and Return Safely to the Side

Equipment

Pool noodle with noodle connector or hula hoop, waterproof digital camera (optional)

Preparation

Use a pool noodle connector to make a circle with the noodles. Create a fun story in which the student is in a photo shoot and needs to smile really big for the camera.

Formation

The student is on the side of the pool with his toes around the edge. An adult spotter stands next him, and the instructor is in chin-deep water approximately 5 feet (1.5 m) from the student.

Instructor Directions

Give safety instructions and cues, and then explain and demonstrate jumping into chin-deep water. Explain to the student that when he is jumping, you will say "1, 2, 3, Smile" and pretend to take a photo with your hands. When the student surfaces and swims back to the wall, hold up the circular noodle or hula hoop (picture frame) and have him imitate the smile he gave as he entered the water as the adult spotter takes a digital photo (if a camera is available).

Student Directions

The student listens to your safety instructions and then performs a feet-first jump into chin-deep water while smiling, surfaces, swims back to the wall, and smiles for the camera through the circular noodle or hoop.

Olympic Jumping Trials

Skill 3.20—Jump Into Chin-Deep Water and Return Safely to the Side

Equipment

Score cards numbered 1 to 10 (optional)

Preparation

Create a fun story in which the student is in the Olympic Trials jumping competition trying to earn a score of 10.

Formation

The student is standing on the edge of the pool with her toes over the edge; an adult spotter is on the deck, and the instructor is in the water.

Instructor Directions

Explain that you are the judge in the Olympic jumping competition. After the student has jumped into chin-deep water and swum back to the side, rate her jump on a scale from 1 to 10. Consider scoring categories such as making a big splash, making a small splash, smiling big, and doing a funny jump. Instead of just saying the number, you can hold scoring cards (just as they do in diving meets).

Student Directions

The student jumps safely into chin-deep water and swims back to the side to see or hear her score. Jump variations can include jumping with her arms crossed or jumping with a funny face.

Treading Water and Recovering From Under Deep Water

Treading water is done in the deep end and consists of sculling with the hands and performing a kick (flutter, egg beater, breaststroke, or scissors kick) to stay in one place and keep the head above water. Students must know how to tread water before swimming in deep water. Knowing at least one of the kicks mentioned earlier and learning sculling with the hands is critical to success in this skill.

Cues for Treading

- Be vertical.
- Stand straight.
- Hold your head up.
- Relax.
- Push your hands out and down; push your hands in and down (scull).
- Kick.

Cues for Recovery From Under Deep Water

- Blow bubbles.
- Look up to the surface.
- Kick, kick, kick.
- Climb a ladder with your hands.
- Push water to the bottom.

Differentiation

- Help the student by physically guiding her toward the surface.
- Provide a very small amount of flotation (e.g., one small square of a multisquare flotation belt).

- Have the student use the steps of an in-wall pool ladder to perform a hand-over-hand climb from underwater.

Freeze Tread

Skill 3.21—Tread in Chin-Deep Water for 10 Seconds

Equipment

Ten- to 20-second segments of music (or a tambourine, drum, or maraca beat) followed by 10- to 20-second segments of silence (on an iPod or MP3 player)

Preparation

None

Formation

The student is standing on tiptoes in chin-deep water. The instructor is sitting on the pool deck 1 to 2 feet (30-60 cm) from the student with music, ready to jump in if needed.

Instructor Directions

Explain and demonstrate the game Freeze Tread, in which the student treads water to the music and then return to tiptoes when the music stops.

Student Directions

Every time the music (or tambourine, drum, or maraca beat) begins, the student starts treading. Once the music stops, she stands on tiptoes and freezes.

Lobster Attack

Skill 3.21—Tread in Chin-Deep Water for 10 Seconds

Equipment

Lobster puppet or stuffed or plastic lobster (optional)

Preparation

Create a fun story in which you are the lobster (or are holding a lobster). When the lobster gets cranky, it nips at anyone holding the gutter or pool edge!

Formation

The student begins by holding on to the pool gutter or edge in chin-deep water; the instructor is lying on the pool deck facing the student.

Instructor Directions

Explain that when you are counting to 10, the student is safe holding on to the gutter; but when you are counting from 11 to 20, he must tread water to avoid the lobster. You can use a stuffed animal or puppet to pretend to gently nip at the student's hands if he is on the gutter during the numbers 11 to 20. Count to 20 several times.

Student Directions

To avoid being nipped during the count from 11 to 20, the student must tread water until the count starts from 1 again and the lobster stops nipping.

Submarine

Skill 3.22—Hang on to the Pool Gutter or Edge in at Least 9 Feet (2.7 m) of Water, Submerge the Full Body, and Recover to the Surface

Equipment

None

Preparation

Create a fun story in which the student is a submarine preparing for submersion and recovery.

Formation

The student is holding the wall in the deep end of the pool.

Instructor Directions

Explain and demonstrate how to bob to your chin five times before submerging about 5 feet (1.5 m) underwater and then use a kick (see cue words) to recover to the surface. Stay close to the student in case she needs assistance, and have a rescue tube available. Cue the student by saying "It's time to charge up the submarine and then submerge."

Student Directions

The student prepares to do the activity by bobbing five times to her chin (charging up) before submerging her entire body in deep water (submarine). Then, using a kick and pulling up on the wall, she resurfaces.

Explorer

Skill 3.23—Hang on to the Pool Gutter or Edge in at Least 9 Feet (2.7 m) of Water, Submerge the Full Body, Release the Gutter or Edge, and Kick Up to the Surface Independently

Equipment

Sinkable toys or other objects

Preparation

This is a lead-up activity to eventually submerge to 9 feet. Submerge toys or objects under water where the pool floor and the pool wall intersect.

Formation

The student is in water (just past the depth where she cannot stand) holding on to the pool wall. Submerged objects are just below her feet.

Instructor Directions

Demonstrate submerging yourself feet-first underwater by pushing down and away from the wall until you reach the pool bottom; then kick up and push water toward the bottom to resurface and grab the wall. Tell the student to try to grab a sinkable object with her toes or hand and bring it to surface.

Student Directions

The student holds the pool wall, slightly lifts herself above the gutter or the edge of the pool, and then pushes up and away from the wall to submerge herself underwater to retrieve an object. She tries to collect as many objects as she can and reports to you each object she finds.

Flipper

Skill 3.23—Hang on to the Pool Gutter or Edge in at Least 9 Feet (2.7 m) of Water, Submerge the Full Body, Release the Gutter or Edge, and Kick Up to the Surface Independently

Equipment

Beach ball

Preparation

Create a fun story in which the student is a dolphin. Explain that dolphins are very talented and smart.

Formation

The student is in water over his head (no more than 9 ft, or 2.7 m) holding and facing the wall.

Instructor Directions

Demonstrate submerging yourself straight down the wall, letting go of the wall, and using your legs to kick up and your arms to climb or push water down to resurface. Then sit on the deck and hold a beach ball over the student's head so he can hit it out of your hands with his head when he resurfaces, like a dolphin in an aquarium show.

Student Directions

The student submerges his entire body underwater, lets go of the wall, kicks and moves his arms to get to the surface, and bumps his head into the ball trying to make it fly as high as possible, like a dolphin.

Introducing the Breaststroke, Backstroke, and Diving

Modified Texas Woman's University Aquatic Assessment: Level 4

Student's name: _____ Instructor's name: _____

Student's date of birth: _____ Date: _____

Page number	Skill number	Skill description	Yes	No	Comments
128	4.1	Bob for one minute in at least 9 feet (2.7 m) of water			
129	4.2	Sidestroke motion with arms, walking 6 yards			
130	4.3	Sidestroke motion with arms, any kick, 12 yards			
131	4.4	Flutter kick 25 yards on front with kickboard			
134	4.5	Float on front for 30 seconds, taking breaths when needed			
135	4.6	Rhythmic breathing to side while leaning forward with hands on knees, for one minute			
136	4.7	Front crawl with arm recovery above the water and rhythmic breathing to the side for 12 yards			
138	4.8	Front crawl with arm recovery above the water and rhythmic breathing to the side for 25 yards			
139	4.9	Float on back for one minute			
140	4.10	Elementary backstroke 12 yards using any kick			
142	4.11	Flutter kick on back for 12 yards			
144	4.12	Backstroke 12 yards with some out-of-water arm recovery			
144	4.13	Backstroke 12 yards with full out-of-water arm recovery			
146	4.14	Swim 6 yards underwater using breaststroke arms			
149	4.15	Use breaststroke arms 12 yards with any kick			

Page number	Skill number	Skill description	Yes	No	Comments
150	4.16	Whip kick 12 yards on front while holding a kickboard towed by the instructor			
151	4.17	Whip kick 12 yards on front while holding a kickboard independently			
151	4.18	Tread in at least 9 feet (2.7 m) of water for one minute			
154	4.19	Kneeling dive into deep water			

General comments:

Modified from Texas Woman's University Aquatic Assessment.

From M. Lepore, L. Columna, and L. Friedlander Litzner, 2015, *Assessments and activities for teaching swimming* (Champaign, IL: Human Kinetics).

Level 4 of the TWU aquatic assessment introduces the skills of the breaststroke, the elementary backstroke, and diving. In this level, students spend the majority of the time in deep water. They are also required to perform the front crawl for longer distances. Most students who are being assessed on level 4 skills (i.e., have mastered level 3 skills) have the breath control, cardiorespiratory endurance, and body control needed for this level.

This level includes 19 skills. As in levels 2 and 3, students perform more advanced versions of some of the skills introduced earlier. Level 4 allows you to assess advanced performances of the front crawl, the backstroke, the elementary backstroke, the breaststroke, bobbing, and floating. The main differences from level 3 are that in level 4 students perform skills for longer distances or periods of time and use more advanced mechanics. In addition, they combine parts of strokes such as breathing and the kick.

Bobbing

In level 3, students bob for a maximum of 20 seconds in chin-deep water. In level 4, they bob longer and in deeper water.

Sponge Man of the Sea

Skill 4.1—Bob for One Minute in at Least 9 Feet (2.7 m) of Water

Equipment

None

Preparation

Visit http://spongebob.nick.com to learn the song to the cartoon *SpongeBob SquarePants.*

Formation

Both the student and the instructor hold the pool gutter or edge in 9 feet (2.7 m) of water.

Instructor Directions

Demonstrate several deep-water bobs away from the pool wall, and then ask the student to do the same. Time the student performing one minute of bobbing while you sing the SpongeBob theme song.

Student Directions

The student pretends to be SpongeBob. While you sing the theme song, the student moves away from the wall into 9 feet (2.7 m) of water, submerges herself (under the sea), and performs bobbing. When she breaks to the surface, shout the lyrics so she can respond "SpongeBob SquarePants!" before going under again.

Sidestroke

The sidestroke allows students to keep their faces out of the water while moving forward. This stroke uses a scissors kick—the top leg moves forward and the bottom leg moves back; then they snap together like scissors. The stroke starts in a side-lying position and, as seen in figure L4.1, the right arm (top arm) is resting along the side of the body with the hand lying on the side of the thigh. As seen in figure L4.1, the left arm (bottom arm) is extended in front with one ear lying on the arm.

To begin the stroke, the bottom arm pulls water toward the chest while the top arm slices through the water in front of the abdomen toward the chin. Then the hand of the top arm rotates to catch water and pushes it past the abdomen, toward the top leg as the bottom arm stretches out to the starting position. In addition, the legs are performing a scissors kick sideways. Once both arms have pushed water backward, the legs have scissored, and the body is back to the starting position, there is a momentary glide (American Red Cross, 2009). This stroke requires the arms and legs to be in harmony and coordinate with each other. This coordination between the arms and the legs occurs when the arms and knees are both bent and when the arms and knees are both straight.

Cues

- Pick the apple.
- Put it in the basket.

Figure L4.1   The sidestroke *(a)* begins in a streamline position on the side, *(b)* with the arm stroke and leg kick beginning about the same time, and ends when the arms and legs return to the starting position.

- Ear in the water.
- Top leg forward.
- Bottom leg back.

Differentiation
- Have the student wear a flotation belt with the clasp part toward the bottom of the pool.
- Have the student lie on a flotation mat to work on the kick.
- Use physical guidance or tactile modeling to help students understand the motions of the stroke.
- Provide additional time for practice sessions.
- Repeat directions and provide additional feedback in small chunks.

Mirror Mirror (Walking)

Skill 4.2—Sidestroke Motion With Arms, Walking 6 Yards

Equipment
None

Preparation
None

Formation

The student and the instructor are in shallow water facing each other.

Instructor Directions

Tell the student that he will be a mirror in this activity and will do the same things that you do. Demonstrate the sidestroke arm motions in a squatting position with your shoulders under water. Tell the student to face you and start mirroring your movements. After you do a few sidestroke arm movements together as a mirror (like a synchronized swimming routine), walk sideways doing the arm motion for 6 yards.

Student Directions

The student mirrors your actions of standing in place and performing the arm motions of the sidestroke. The student faces the instructor, and both walk sideways for 6 yeards mirroring the sidestroke arm movement.

Mirror Mirror (Swimming)

Skill 4.3—Sidestroke Motion With Arms, Any Kick, 12 Yards

Equipment

None

Preparation

None

Formation

The student and the instructor are in shallow water facing each other.

Instructor Directions

Tell the student that she will be a mirror in this activity and will do the same things that you do. Demonstrate the sidestroke arm motions in a squatting position with your shoulders underwater. After you do a few sidestroke arms together as a mirror (like a synchronized swimming routine), push off the bottom of the pool and swim the sidestroke facing each other for 12 yards. You should be about 5 feet apart so as not to bump into each other.

Student Directions

The student stands facing you in shallow water and mirrors your actions of standing in place and doing the arm motions of the sidestroke. She then imitates you gently pushing off the bottom of the pool to lie on her side and practice the arm motion of the sidestroke swimming facing you, about 5 feet away from you.

Flutter Kick

In level 3, students perform the flutter kick with instructor assistance and independently for 12 yards. In level 4, they perform the flutter kick for 25 yards using a kickboard.

Red Light, Green Light, 1, 2, 3

Skill 4.4—Flutter Kick 25 Yards on Front With Kickboard

Equipment
Kickboards (one per student)

Preparation
None

Formation
The instructor is in waist- or chest-deep water at the pool wall 25 yards from the students and facing away from them. Remember that all activities must be supervised by a lifeguard on deck.

Instructor Directions
Demonstrate the flutter kick with a kickboard and explain that when you turn away and shout "Red light, green light, 1, 2, 3," they should flutter kick on their kickboards to try to reach you. When you say "3," you will turn to face them and they must have stopped moving forward. If you do this activity in the deep end of the pool, students should tread water. If you do the activity in the shallow end, students should stand up. They can start to move forward again when you turn your back and begin repeating the phrase. The first one to reach you will become the next leader to call "Red light, green light, 1, 2, 3."

Student Directions
When your back is turned, the students perform the front flutter kick using their kickboards and move toward you. When you finish saying "Red light, green light, 1, 2, 3" and turn around, they must stand up or tread water with no forward movement. The game continues until one student taps you on the shoulder and becomes the leader.

Colors

Skill 4.4—Flutter Kick 25 Yards on Front With Kickboard

Equipment
Two kickboards of different colors (one kickboard per student)

Preparation
Each student is assigned a color by the instructor and is told to remember their color.

Formation
Students are standing in chest-deep water, 12 yards away from the wall, holding a kickboard. The instructor has a kickboard and is 5 yards behind the group, facing their backs.

Instructor Directions

Review the proper use of a kickboard and an efficient front flutter kick. Explain that you are the "Color Catcher" and will be calling out a color (one of the two colors of the kickboards) and will try to catch the students who have that color kickboard as they flutter kick to the pool wall 12 yards away. You should kick using a kickboard and attempt to tag as many students as possible as they kick toward the wall. A tagged student must finish kicking to the wall with his face in the water, doing rhythmic breathing. Once the group is all at the wall, you and all swimmers kick back to the starting point and the second colored kickboard group gets to play.

Student Directions

Students whose color was called flutter kick with a kickboard to the wall 12 yards away while trying to avoid getting tagged by you. If a student gets tagged, he must continue to kick to the wall with rhythmic breathing. Once the group gets to the wall, they should flutter kick back to join the other color group and wait until their next turn. The game will be repeated as time and tiredness allow.

Floating Ring Scramble

Skill 4.4—Flutter Kick 25 Yards on Front With Kickboard

Equipment

Floating rings, kickboards (one per student)

Preparation

Place floating rings on the pool surface 25 yards from the students.

Formation

Students line up in waist- or chest-level water on the wall 25 yards from the floating objects.

Instructor Directions

Demonstrate kicking with a kickboard toward a ring, picking it up, and bringing it back to the pool deck on your kickboard. Explain that the goal of the race is to collect as many rings as possible. Blow a whistle to start the game.

Student Directions

When the whistle blows, students kick (using kickboards) to collect as many floating rings as possible. The students must balance the floating rings on their kickboards to bring them back to the side of the pool. Only one object can be collected at a time.

Matching Eggs

Skill 4.4—Flutter Kick 25 Yards on Front With Kickboard

Equipment

Plastic eggs that separate in half (six per student), kickboards

Preparation

Separate the eggs and place the halves on the water 25 yards from the students.

Formation

Students line up with their backs to the wall in waist- or chest-level water while holding kickboards.

Instructor Directions

Demonstrate the front flutter kick using a kickboard. Tell the students to kick 25 yards to collect enough egg pieces to make six eggs (12 pieces, total). Students will have to balance the egg pieces on their kickboards, bring them to the start, and put the eggs together. You can consider timing how long it takes each student to assemble six eggs.

Student Directions

The students kick 25 yards to the floating egg halves and collect enough egg halves to make six eggs (at least 12 pieces), bring them to the start by balancing them on their kickboards, and put the eggs together.

Floating

In level 2, students float on their fronts and backs with instructor support and independently up to five seconds. In level 4, they float on their fronts for 30 seconds, taking breaths when needed. In addition, they must float on their backs for one minute.

Cues for the Back Float

- Head back
- Ears in water
- Chin up
- Arms and legs out
- Belly up

Cues for the Front Float

- Nose toward the floor
- Arms and legs out
- Belly down

Differentiation

- Provide physical guidance to students who need it.
- Allow the student to use several pool noodles and remove one at a time as the student progresses.
- Provide flotation under a body part that is the densest.
- Let the student hold a floating barbell in each hand or have one under each armpit.
- Use inexpensive blow-up rafts somewhat deflated for support.

- Provide extra attention and repeat directions when necessary.
- Provide directions or pictures of the activity on a whiteboard in the students' lane.
- Provide braille directions.
- Allow for preferred seating during demonstrations.
- Have an assistant in the water.

ABC Float

Skill 4.5—Float on Front for 30 Seconds, Taking Breaths When Needed

Equipment
Clock or stopwatch

Preparation
None

Formation
The instructor is standing near the students, who are scattered around standing in chest-deep water.

Instructor Directions
Explain and demonstrate a 30-second front float, showing the students how you can lift your face out of the water to breathe and put it back down, without putting your feet down to touch the pool bottom. When the students are performing the front float, start saying or singing the alphabet loudly. Do this loudly enough that when the student picks her head up to breathe, she hears the letter you are saying so she can see how long she floated before coming up for a breath (attempting to make it through the whole alphabet, which you will time to equal floating for 30 seconds). Please remind the students to blow bubbles when their faces are in the water and to take a breath every few seconds.

Student Directions
The student does a front float while listening to you saying or singing the alphabet. Every few seconds (maybe every 5 letters), she should come up for a breath without putting her feet down.

Rhythmic Breathing

Rhythmic breathing uses a coordinated cadence of breathing in when the mouth is out of the water, and blowing bubbles when the face is in the water during aquatic skills and swim strokes. Rhythmic breathing is critical to the improvement of swim strokes on the front. Once students have their faces in the water and can perform correct rhythmic breathing, they are better able to maintain proper body position.

Cues for Rhythmic Breathing for the Front Crawl

- With ear in water, breathe in.
- Nose points to the pool bottom; blow bubbles.
- Hum (air will come out of the nose so water will not go in).

Differentiation

- Use jog belts and pool noodles under the hips.
- Provide fins, which strengthen the kick, helping the student's face come out of the water.
- Provide verbal cues for when to turn the head, giving physical assistance as needed.
- Use braille or large print on visual information.
- Use auditory sounds for targets.
- Substitute arm motions for leg motions if necessary, and vice versa.
- Use sign language or hand gestures if necessary.
- Post laminated written descriptions of the activities, and provide cues for further understanding.

Talk to the Hand

Skill 4.6—Rhythmic Breathing to Side While Leaning Forward With Hands on Knees, for One Minute

Equipment

None

Preparation

None

Formation

The student is in waist-deep water with his hands on his knees facing the instructor.

Instructor Directions

In waist-deep water, place your hands on your knees, and place one side of your face and one ear in the water. Demonstrate rhythmic breathing, taking a breath in, rotating your face toward the bottom of the pool and blowing bubbles, keeping the back of the head above water, and then rotating your face to the side again to take another breath. Let the student know that you will put your hand about 12 inches (30 cm) below where the student will be putting her face in the water and instruct her to perform rhythmic breathing for one minute. When her face is in the water, she should shout out a favorite phrase from a song to your hand (talk to the hand) while blowing bubbles underwater or you can also hold out a certain number of fingers underwater and have the student call out the number of fingers that are held.

Student Directions

The student puts her hands on her knees and performs stationary rhythmic breathing. When her face is in the water, she shouts out a favorite phrase from a song or the number of fingers you are holding out.

Front Crawl With Rhythmic Breathing

In level 3, students perform the front crawl for 12 yards using rhythmic breathing. In level 4, students swim up to 25 yards using rhythmic breathing to the side and recovering (when the hand returns to the front after the stroke) their arms out of the water.

Cues

- Keep your body horizontal.
- Breathe to the side.
- Keep your elbows high.
- Roll your body.
- Reach forward.
- Pull back toward your pocket.
- Kick to boil water.

Differentiation

- Students can use jog belts, pool noodles under their hips, fins to help with kicking, verbal cues, or physical assistance as needed.
- Use braille or large print on visual information. Use auditory sounds for targets.
- Allow students to substitute arm motions for leg motions if necessary, or vice versa.
- Use sign language or hand gestures if necessary.
- Post laminated written description of activities, as well as the cues to further students' understanding.

Hum It

Skill 4.7—Front Crawl With Arm Recovery Above the Water and Rhythmic Breathing to the Side for 12 Yards

Equipment

None

Preparation

None

Formation

The student is in waist- or chest-deep water with his back to the pool wall, and the instructor is 12 yards away.

Instructor Directions

Demonstrate the front crawl with rhythmic breathing to the side emphasizing that when the face is in the water the student should blow bubbles by humming. Say "Hum it" to signal to the student to begin swimming and humming his favorite song.

Student Directions

On the signal "Hum it," the student begins to front crawl toward you. While he is swimming the front crawl, he should be doing rhythmic breathing. The student should hum his favorite song while blowing bubbles with his face in the water.

Read It

Skill 4.7—Front Crawl With Arm Recovery Above the Water and Rhythmic Breathing to the Side for 12 Yards

Equipment

Laminated cards with letters on them

Preparation

Create laminated cards with letters on them that spell out a word.

Formation

The student is in the water with her back to the wall. The instructor is on the pool deck.

Instructor Directions

Demonstrate a front crawl for 12 yards with rhythmic breathing to the side. Explain to the student that she will be looking for letters you will hold up each time she turns her head to the side to breathe. (Use verbal cues for students who can't see.) Tell her the letters will spell a word that she can tell you when she finishes swimming. Stress that she should focus on rhythmically breathing to the side.

Student Directions

The student does the front crawl breathing to the left and looks for the letters you hold up each time she turns. She then tells you the word the letters spelled out when she finishes her swim. She then repeats the drill to the right side.

Olympic Trials

Skill 4.7—Front Crawl With Arm Recovery Above the Water and Rhythmic Breathing to the Side for 12 Yards

Equipment

Stopwatch, personalized reward, record book

Preparation

Create a medal for an award ceremony (e.g., laminated paper), or have another type of reward on hand, as well as a record book.

Formation

The student starts at one end of the pool, and the instructor is at the other end, if the pool length is 12 yards. If the pool is longer than 12 yards, the instructor waits at the 12-yard point. If the pool is shorter than 12 yards, the student swims until he has covered 12 yards in waist- or chest-deep water.

Instructor Directions

Explain that this activity is a chance to record the student's 12-yard front crawl time in the record book. Then give him the signal to start, time his swim, and record it in a record book. This timed swim can be done on a regular basis, and the student can receive a medal or an award every time he beats his record.

Student Directions

On your signal, the student swims 12 yards using the front crawl with arm recovery above the water and rhythmic breathing to the side. The goal is to swim a personal record while using correct technique.

What to Watch

Skill 4.8—Front Crawl With Arm Recovery Above the Water and Rhythmic Breathing to the Side for 25 Yards

Equipment

None

Preparation

None

Formation

The student and the instructor are in any depth of water, each holding the pool wall with one hand.

Instructor Directions

Watch the student swim 25 yards and ask her to identify one part of her stroke that she would like to improve (e.g., elbow movement). After she has swum 25 yards, give her feedback about the part of the stroke she wants to improve. Then switch roles and ask the student to watch a particular aspect of your stroke (e.g., kicking). Consider doing something a little wrong for the student to identify. If your mechanics are not correct, the student needs to let you know and also tell you how the mechanics should be.

Student Directions

The student chooses one part of her stroke for you to watch as she performs the front crawl for 25 yards. After you give her feedback, tell her what part of your stroke to watch while you swim 25 yards. She reports on that aspect of your stroke, including how to fix anything that was wrong.

Shipwreck

Skill 4.9—Float on Back for One Minute

Equipment
Clock or stopwatch

Preparation
None

Formation
The student is in deep water (where he can't touch the floor) facing the wall.

Instructor Directions
On the signal "Ships afloat," the student lets go of the wall, leans his head back, and assumes the back float position. After one minute, say "Shipwreck," which is the signal for the student to curl up in a ball and sink and then return to the surface to end the activity.

Student Directions
When the student hears "Ships afloat," he assumes the back float position for one minute. When he hears "Shipwreck," he curls up in a ball and sinks and then returns to the surface to end the activity.

Elementary Backstroke

The elementary backstroke is a resting stroke that does not require much energy. The arm motion is done underwater in a relaxed manner, with the arms starting at the sides of the body. The fingers slide upward toward the armpits (like a monkey scratching his armpits) as the elbows bend (see figure L4.2*a*). Then the student extends the fingertips out, so that the arms form the top of the letter T (like an airplane). Then the student pushes the water toward the feet with the whole arm and ends with the arms down to the sides (soldier). This last movement is done simultaneously with a whip kick that moves the student forward toward the head.

Cues
- Belly up, head back
- Zip up zippers on each side of the body, tickle armpits, arms like a T (or an airplane), arms like a soldier
- Monkey, airplane, soldier

Differentiation
- Provide tactile modeling or physical guidance.
- Have the student perform the monkey, airplane, and soldier motions while lying on the deck first.

- Repeat directions and cue words during the physical movements.
- Use cue cards and pictures at various intervals during the instruction.
- Use a flotation belt on the student's waist.

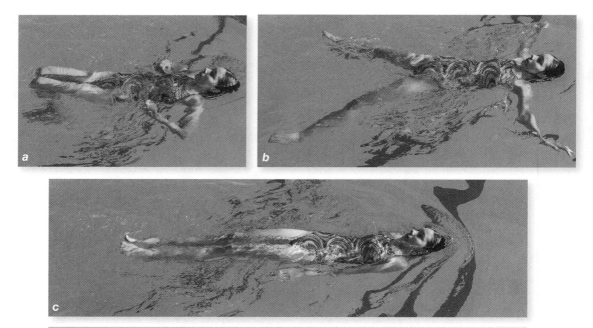

Figure L4.2   To help students learn the elementary backstroke, cue them to be *(a)* a monkey by trailing the fingers up the side and dropping the heels of the feet to the bottom of the pool, *(b)* an airplane by extending fingertips out to the side while rotating the heels of the feet out, and *(c)* a soldier by returning arms and legs to go back to streamline position.

Monkey, Airplane, Soldier

Skill 4.10—Elementary Backstroke 12 Yards Using Any Kick

Equipment
None

Preparation
None

Formation
The student and the instructor stand facing each other on the pool deck.

Instructor Directions
Demonstrate and verbalize the cues for the elementary backstroke (monkey, airplane, soldier) while standing on the pool deck. Perform the moves with the student on the deck and then in the water for 12 yards.

Student Directions

The student watches you demonstrate the elementary backstroke while standing on the deck reciting the cues (monkey, airplane, soldier). He then repeats the cues (monkey, airplane, soldier) in a rhythmic pattern while imitating the motions. The student should hold the soldier position for three seconds. When you believe she is ready, she performs the stroke in the pool for 12 yards. Note that she can use any kick in this activity; the arm motion is most important at this time.

Backward High Fives

Skill 4.10—Elementary Backstroke 12 Yards Using Any Kick

Equipment
None

Preparation
None

Formation
The student is in waist- to chest-deep water facing the wall with the instructor behind his head.

Instructor Directions
Demonstrate a back glide off the wall and then use the arm motion of the elementary backstroke (monkey, airplane, soldier). Then stand behind the student and put your hands where the student's hands will be during the airplane segment of the arm motion. When the student performs that part of the stroke, she gently hits your hands with the backs of her hands, like giving two backward high fives. The instructor must jog backward after the high five so as to not get in the way of the student.

Student Directions
The student pushes off the wall into a back glide and performs the arm motions of the elementary backstroke. When she extends her arms like an airplane, she taps the back of your hands (like giving two backward high fives).

The swimmer gives a backward high five to the instructor when she puts her arms in the airplane position.

Can You?

Skill 4.11—Flutter Kick on Back for 12 Yards

Equipment
Kickboard

Preparation
None

Formation
The student and the instructor are in chest-deep water.

Instructor Directions
Demonstrate the backstroke kick for 12 yards. Then give the student challenges such as the following:

- Can you . . . hold the kickboard with two hands and kick on your back for 12 yards?
- Can you . . . hold the kickboard with one hand and kick on your back for 12 yards?
- Can you . . . put both arms above your head and kick on your back for 12 yards?
- Can you . . . put one arm above your head and kick on your back for 12 yards?

Student Directions
The student swims or kicks 12 yards on her back performing the challenges presented by the instructor.

Backstroke

The backstroke is a long axis stroke. This means the body rotates on an imaginary axis from head to toe. The arm comes out of the water straight and bends to push water toward the feet once underneath the water (see figure L4.3). The head stays relatively still while the arms move in opposition, and the body rotates so that the shoulder of the arm out of the water rotates to point to the ceiling. The backstroke uses the flutter kick. Cues for the backstroke depend on the proficiency and cognitive level of the student.

Cues for the Backstroke (Novice Level)
- Big arms
- Chin up

Cues for the Backstroke (Intermediate Level)
- Pole going through your body from your head to your toes
- Thumb out, pinky in
- Little knees give more

Figure L4.3 The backstroke uses alternating arm motions with a flutter kick.

Cues for the Backstroke (Advanced Level)
- Shoulders rotate
- Hips up and body roll

Differentiation
- Provide physical assistance or flotation assistance if necessary.
- Have a student use fins for better propulsion; provide physical guidance for the arms.
- Have the student hold on to the pool gutter or edge with one hand and concentrate on one arm at a time.
- Have the student walk 12 yards using alternating (one at a time) backward arm movements.
- Provide a separate area for those with attention challenges.
- Use a cone or rope off an area that is 12 by 12 yards.
- Provide written, pictorial, or braille directions as needed.

Broken Fan

Skill 4.12—Backstroke 12 Yards With Some Out-of-Water Arm Recovery

Equipment
None

Preparation
None

Formation
The student is in chest-deep water.

Instructor Directions
Ask the student to visualize a fan with only one blade. Then demonstrate pushing off the wall and doing the backstroke with only one arm for 12 yards. Have the student push off the wall on her back and do the backstroke while pretending she is a broken fan. Then have her do the same with the other arm. Point out that the student will have to work hard in order to stay straight within the water.

Student Directions
The student pushes off the wall on her back and does the backstroke while pretending to be a broken fan (i.e., with only one arm working). She does this with each arm and then tells you what she noticed about how she moved in the water. She should notice that she must work hard in order to stay straight within the water.

Who Can? You Can!

Skill 4.13—Backstroke 12 Yards With Full Out-of-Water Arm Recovery

Equipment
None

Preparation
None

Formation
All students are spread out in the pool in chest-deep water.

Instructor Directions
Demonstrate the backstroke for 12 yards. Then give the students the following challenges:

- Who can swim the backstroke 12 yards?
- Who can swim the backstroke 12 yards without letting their hips sink?
- Who can swim the backstroke 12 yards while looking at the ceiling the whole time?
- Who can swim the backstroke 12 yards without getting water in their nose?

- Who can swim the backstroke 12 yards while kicking with floppy feet (ankles relaxed)?
- Who can swim the backstroke 12 yards while keeping their arms straight when they're out of the water?
- Who can swim the backstroke 12 yards with their thumbs exiting the water first and their pinkies entering the water first?
- Who can start with their feet on the ground, lie back in the water, float for five seconds on their back, and then do the backstroke for 12 yards?

Student Directions

The students swim the backstroke 12 yards at a time in response to your challenges.

Underwater Swimming Using Modified Breaststroke Arms

Swimming underwater is a skill many students can do before they can perform traditional swim strokes. Being efficient underwater swimmers requires that the swimmer kicks using any type of kick, and with the arms use a sweeping motion like opening curtains from the middle and pushing them away so you can look out the window. This is somewhat like the breaststroke arm motion (see breaststroke arm motion description in level 5). In this book we will call wide sweeping arms the modified breaststroke arm motion (because the arms sweep out farther than they do in the traditional breaststroke—see figure L4.4).

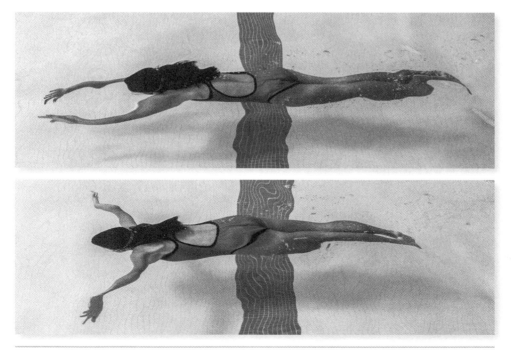

Figure L4.4   Arms sweep out further than the traditional breaststroke arms when swimming underwater.

Cues

- Big pull
- Arms shoot forward
- Kick, kick, kick

Differentiation

- Have the student wear fins.
- Have the student not go very far underwater.
- Use tactile modeling by having the student put his hands on your arms or legs and participate along with you.
- Provide physical assistance.
- Use ropes or buoys for tactile orientation.

Tunnels

Skill 4.14—Swim 6 Yards Underwater Using Breaststroke Arms

Equipment

Two extra-large hula hoops, light weights, 12-inch nylon rope

Preparation

Submerge two extra-large hula hoops connected to the nylon rope and the weights.

Formation

The student stands with her back against the pool wall in shallow water. The instructor is standing next to two hula hoops vertically submerged underwater.

Instructor Directions

Review the breaststroke arm cues and demonstrate the technique. Challenge the student to swim underwater through the hoop of her choice. Have her repeat until it is no longer a challenge. You can arrange the hula hoops so that they are farther apart or in different directions to increase the challenge.

Student Directions

The student swims through the submerged hula hoops using a modified breaststroke (the arms sweep out farther than they do in the traditional breaststroke) arm action and any kick.

Tunnel Tag

Skill 4.14—Swim 6 Yards Underwater Using Breaststroke Arms

Equipment

Three extra-large hula hoops, three light weights, three pieces of 12-inch nylon rope

After gliding through the hoops, the swimmer will sweep her arms wide to swim underwater.

Preparation
Submerge three extra-large hula hoops, each connected to the nylon ropes and a weight.

Formation
The students and the instructor are in the shallow end.

Instructor Directions
Demonstrate jogging while using the breaststroke arms and also swimming underwater using the breaststroke arms. Begin a game of tag while jogging using the breaststroke arms. Then tell the students that when they are tagged they must swim through the hula hoops using the breaststroke arms to get back in the game.

Student Directions
The students run in shallow water doing the breaststroke arm motion to flee the tagger and avoid getting tagged. If tagged, they must swim through the hula hoops and swim underwater using breaststroke arms to get back in the game.

Breaststroke With Any Kick

The breaststroke is one of the four competitive strokes; however, in a recreational form, it can be used as a resting stroke. It consists of symmetrical arm action, a breath to the front, a whip kick with the knees staying toward the inside of the ankles, and a coordination of body parts (synchronizing arms, legs, and breathing) that is often cued as "Pull, breathe, kick, glide." The breaststroke is performed facedown in the water without rotating the torso. The arms stay in the water and move synchronously, while the legs perform a whip (frog) kick (see figure L4.5). It is possible to keep the head elevated out of the water throughout the stroke (American Red Cross, 2009). However, the correct form is to put the face in the water and blow bubbles from the start of the kick and into the glide.

Cues for the Breaststroke (Novice)
- Scoop the ice cream and breathe.
- Give the ice cream to a friend.
- Kick water back with the soles of your feet.

Figure L4.5   The breaststroke is performed facedown in the water without rotating the torso.

Cues for the Breaststroke (Intermediate)
- Pull/breathe, kick/glide.
- Clap the bottoms of the feet together.

Cues for the Breaststroke (Advanced)
- Fast pull (no pause), long glide.
- Stretch to breathe.
- Chin down.
- Kick and undulate.

Differentiation
- Provide additional instruction on land if necessary.
- Have the student practice the kick with the upper body (waist up) on a floating mat.
- Use physical guidance to move the student's feet or hands through their proper range of motion.
- Draw a picture of the shape the arms form (backwards heart) and of what the legs are doing.

Draw a Heart

Skill 4.15—Use Breaststroke Arms 12 Yards With Any Kick

Equipment
Laminated cutout of a heart (optional, if student needs help with the shape and size)

Preparation
None

Formation
The student is in chest-deep water with the instructor standing next to him.

Instructor Directions
Demonstrate breaststroke arms and draw an upside-down heart in the air, on the student's back, and on the water surface with both arms at the same time.

Student Directions
After watching the demonstration, the student traces an upside-down heart on the pool wall with both hands at the same time. Then she walks toward the instructor drawing upside-down hearts on the water surface. The student then swims toward the instructor, who is 12 yards away, performing the breaststroke pull. (Any kick is acceptable at this time because the focus is on the arm movement.)

Whip Kick

The whip kick is used in the breaststroke and elementary backstroke. This kick uses the bottoms of the feet to propel the student in the opposite direction. Students must symmetrically dorsiflex the feet (bend the ankles to move the feet toward the head), bend the knees, and rotate the feet out to the side; then "whip" the lower leg around and point the toes so that the feet come together while pushing the water backward (see figure L4.6).

Cues
- Knees are shoulder-width apart.
- Bend the knees and ankles.
- Whip the legs around.
- Grab the water with your toes.
- Point your toes, legs together.

Differentiation
- Provide additional practice by having the students lie on their fronts (on the deck) and dangle their legs over the side of the pool.
- Use flotation devices to help students concentrate on the body position and kick.

Figure L4.6   On the whip kick on the front, the swimmer *(a)* brings the heels toward the bottom and rotates feet out to the side; then *(b)* the legs whip around and push the water backwards with the bottom of the feet.

Hang It Up

Skill 4.16—Whip Kick 12 Yards on Front While Holding a Kickboard Towed by the Instructor

Equipment
Plastic floating rings, flexible ring toss stick, kickboard

Preparation
Have a ring toss stick set up on the deck 6 yards from the student. Scatter rings around the pool.

Formation
The student is in waist- or chest-level water with his back to the pool wall holding a kickboard. The instructor is with him in the water.

Instructor Directions
After demonstrating the whip kick, the instructor tows the student, who is holding the kickboard and propelling himself using the whip kick. While you are towing the student, have him retrieve the floating rings; then tow him to the ring toss stick to toss them on.

Student Directions

The student uses a kickboard and kicks 6-yard segments with your assistance to retrieve rings from the water, balance them on his kickboard, and bring them one at a time to the ring toss stick. After tossing a ring onto the stick, the student continues to travel in 6-yard segments to retrieve more rings until they are all on the stick.

Under the Arches

Skill 4.17—Whip Kick 12 Yards on Front While Holding a Kickboard Independently

Equipment

Two pool noodles, kickboard

Preparation

Wedge one end of each pool noodle into the gutter or rest it in the pool deck and hold the other ends in the water to form two arches about 12 yards from the student.

Formation

The student is in waist- or chest-level water with a kickboard. The instructor is holding one end of each of two pool noodles to form two arches 12 yards from the student.

Instructor Directions

Instruct the student to use her kickboard and practice the whip kick as she swims under the arches.

Student Directions

The student uses her kickboard to practice the whip kick while swimming under the arches.

Treading

In level 3, students tread water in chin-deep water for 10 seconds. In this level, students must tread water for longer periods of time and in deeper water.

Going on a Swimming Trip

Skill 4.18—Tread in at Least 9 Feet (2.7 m) of Water for One Minute

Equipment

None

Preparation

Create a list in your head of items that could be brought on a swimming trip that begin with the letters A through Z.

Formation

The student is in the deep end of the pool holding the gutter.

Instructor Directions

Demonstrate the critical cues of treading water, and tell the student that when you say "Go," he will push off the wall and tread water for 60 seconds. While treading, he is to say "I'm going on a swimming trip and I am going to bring . . ." and then name something that begins with the letter A. You then repeat the phrase and the student's word and add something that begins with the letter B (e.g., "I'm going on a swimming trip, and I am going to bring an apple and a beach towel"). Continue going back and forth with the student and adding words in alphabetical order until the 60 seconds of treading is over. Make sure the student is safe in the water.

Student Directions

The student treads water for 60 seconds while going back and forth with you naming things to bring on a swimming trip in alphabetical order.

Kneeling Dive

Diving consists of entering the water hands first, followed by the head, trunk, and legs. Many students have difficulty entering the water upside down. Before undertaking lessons in diving, make sure students can recover from deep water and maintain a streamlined position, and have good listening behaviors to prevent wild and impulsive entries into dangerous areas of the pool. The goal is to break the surface of the water with their hands and then have the rest of the body enter though that same point. Diving must be taught by an instructor with experience in teaching diving and must be conducted in a pool that is at least 9 feet (2.7 m) deep. Diving should never be taught in an above-ground pool.

In a kneeling dive, the student starts by getting in a kneeling position by placing one knee on the deck of the pool with the supporting leg's toe pointedThe front leg's foot is at the edge of the pool with the toes curled around the edge of the pool. The student tucks her chin; squeezes her ears with her upper arms; places hands together, one on top of the other, and extends them towards the water, pointing at a spot in the water about 2 feet (0.61 m) from the edge of the pool; and angles herself towards the water (see figure L4.7a). The student then slowly extends her front knee, keeping her chin down with hands pointed to the water. She then tips into the water, with hands touching the water first. As she enters, the legs should straighten and meet so that she enters the water straight like a pencil.

Cues for Diving: Water Entry
- Streamlined position
- Chin down
- Hand grab hand
- Legs together
- Tight body
- Use legs to push

Figure L4.7   In a kneeling dive, *(a)* the toes of the lead foot are curled around the edge of the pool and arms extended toward the water, then *(b)* the swimmer begins to enter the water with straight arms and chin tucked, pushing the legs straight so that *(c)* the body is in a pencil-straight position going into the water.

Differentiation

- Substitute sliding down a wet mat in place of a dive from the deck.
- Substitute an in-water surface dive in place of a dive from the deck.
- Substitute jumping instead of diving from the deck for those with neck issues.

Ring of Fire

Skill 4.19—Kneeling Dive Into Deep Water

Equipment

Two pool noodles, two noodle connectors, cushiony bath mat

Preparation

Use two pool noodles and connectors to form a large circle.

Formation

The instructor is in the deep end of the pool (at least 9 ft, or 2.7 m) holding the pool noodle circle 5 feet (1.5 m) from the edge of the pool. The student is kneeling on the bath mat at the edge of the pool facing the instructor.

Instructor Directions

After demonstrating a proper kneeling dive and explaining the safety rules of diving, the instructor stays in the water, holding the circular pool noodle 5 feet from the edge of the pool. Tell the student to perform a kneeling dive through the circular noodle. Remind her to place her hands to aim for the center of the noodle circle (the ring of fire).

Student Directions

The student performs a kneeling dive through the ring of fire trying not to touch it.

Skee-Dive

Skill 4.19—Kneeling Dive Into Deep Water

Equipment

Four pool noodles, four noodle connectors, cushiony bath mat

Preparation

Make two large circles by connecting two noodles with foam noodle connectors. Place the bath mat at the edge of the pool.

Formation

The instructor is in the deep end of the pool (at least 9 ft, or 2.7 m). The student is kneeling on a cushiony bath mat at the edge of the pool facing the instructor.

Instructor Directions

Place one large noodle circle close to the pool wall (3 ft, or 1 m) and the other a little farther away (5 ft, or 1.5 m). Tell the student that he can do a kneeling dive through either circle. Explain that the goal is to score 25 points after five dives, and that the closer circle is worth 5 points and the farther circle is worth 10 points.

Student Directions

The student tries to score 25 points in five dives by doing kneeling dives through either circle.

Learning the Front Crawl, Backstroke, Breaststroke, and Sidestroke

Modified Texas Woman's University Aquatic Assessment: Level 5

Student's name: _____ Instructor's name: _____

Student's date of birth: _____ Date: _____

Page number	Skill number	Skill description	Yes	No	Comments
157	5.1	Front crawl for 12 yards with rhythmic breathing, high elbows, and body roll			
159	5.2	Front crawl for 25 yards with rhythmic breathing, high elbows, and body roll			
162	5.3	Backstroke for 12 yards with above-the-water recovery			
164	5.4	Backstroke for 25 yards with above-the-water recovery			
166	5.5	Elementary backstroke with whip kick for 12 yards			
167	5.6	Elementary backstroke with whip kick for 25 yards			
168	5.7	Breaststroke with whip kick for 12 yards			
169	5.8	Breaststroke with whip kick for 25 yards			
169	5.9	Tread in at least 9 feet (2.7 m) of water for two minutes			
172	5.10	Sidestroke for 12 yards using the scissors kick			
172	5.11	Sidestroke for 25 yards using the scissors kick			

General comments:

Modified from Texas Woman's University Aquatic Assessment.

From M. Lepore, L. Columna, and L. Friedlander Litzner, 2015, *Assessments and activities for teaching swimming* (Champaign, IL: Human Kinetics).

evel 5 skills consist of all of the skills that students need to successfully and safely participate in aquatic environments. For the most part, once students pass level 5, they can participate in novice competitive swimming events and take part in more advanced aquatic activities such as beginner water polo, paddleboarding, and other sports for which swimming ability is a prerequisite. The 11 skills in level 5 include the front crawl, backstroke, breaststroke, and sidestroke.

Front Crawl

In level 4, students performed the front crawl with arm recovery above the water and with rhythmic breathing to the side for 25 yards. This level prepares students for competitive sports or advanced swimming skills by having them perform the front crawl for a distance of 25 yards with rhythmic breathing, high elbows, and body roll. Because body roll is a more advanced component of the front crawl, students will perform it for 12 yards before moving to 25 yards.

Out of the Gate

Skill 5.1—Front Crawl for 12 Yards With Rhythmic Breathing, High Elbows, and Body Roll

Equipment
Kickboard, something to mark a finish line

Preparation
Mark a finish line 12 yards from the wall.

Formation
The instructor is standing next to the student holding a kickboard in front of the student like a gate. The student is holding on to the wall in waist- or chest-deep water, with one foot on the wall waiting for the command to start swimming.

Instructor Directions
Hold the kickboard in front of the student, say "Take your mark, Go," and lift the kickboard up (open the gate) as the student swims the front crawl with high elbows and body roll to the finish line 12 yards away.

Student Directions
The student starts with her foot on the wall, holding the wall with one hand and pointing the other hand toward the finish line. On the command "Go," the student pushes off the wall and swims the front crawl to the finish line with high elbows and body roll.

Swim to Win

Skill 5.1—Front Crawl for 12 Yards With Rhythmic Breathing, High Elbows, and Body Roll

Equipment
None

Preparation
None

Formation
The student starts 12 yards from the wall in waist- or chest-level water, facing the instructor, who is standing at the wall.

Instructor Directions
You are the judge for this competition. As the student swims 12 yards, observe the stroke and give 1 point for each of the criteria presented in the front crawl skill description in level 3: keep your body horizontal, breathe to the side, keep your elbows high, roll your body, reach forward, pull back toward your pocket, and kick to boil water. The highest score is 7.

Student Directions
When you say "Go," the student swims the front crawl toward the wall, attempting to follow all seven cues for the front crawl.

Catch Up

Skill 5.1—Front Crawl for 12 Yards With Rhythmic Breathing, High Elbows, and Body Roll

Equipment
None

Preparation
None

Formation
The student starts in waist- or chest-deep water at the wall with 12 yards of clear space in front of him.

Instructor Directions
Demonstrate the "catch up" arm motion of gliding off the wall with one hand on top of the other and arms extended. Using the flutter kick and the front crawl arm motions, stroke with one arm (with a high elbow and body roll) and touch the hand of the other arm before beginning to stroke with that arm. Have the student perform this stroke, and provide feedback when necessary.

In the Catch Up activity, the swimmer *(a)* performs a one-arm front crawl and then *(b)* catches the other hand before the next one-arm stroke.

Student Directions

The student swims 12 yards using the flutter kick and a "catch up" front crawl arm motion while breathing to the side. He alternates arms using high elbows and body roll and keeps one arm out straight while stroking normally with the other. The student may not move the extended arm to pull normally until the other arm comes back to the starting position and taps the waiting hand.

Olympic Tryouts

Skill 5.2—Front Crawl for 25 Yards With Rhythmic Breathing, High Elbows, and Body Roll

Equipment

Stopwatch, a place to record times (e.g., notebook, iPad)

Preparation

At least two students are needed for this activity.

Formation

One swimmer is on either end of the pool, holding the wall.

Instructor Directions

Explain that the students will do a relay where one swimmer performs the front crawl with high elbows and body roll for the length of the pool, then touches the hand of the waiting swimmer. The other swimmer then does the same toward the other end. Record students' times to track their improvements.

Student Directions

The students participate in the relay race with the understanding that they are trying only to beat their own previous records.

Best Average

Skill 5.2—Front Crawl for 25 Yards With Rhythmic Breathing, High Elbows, and Body Roll

Equipment

Stopwatch, a place to record times (e.g., notebook, iPad)

Preparation

None

Formation

The student is in any depth of water with his back to the wall, one hand holding the gutter or the edge of the pool, one foot against the wall, and 25 yards of clear space in front of him.

Instructor Directions

Explain to the student that he will swim using the front crawl with high elbows and body roll for four 25-yard segments and be timed for each one. Provide rest breaks between segments as needed. Time each attempt and average the four attempts. After the trials, discuss with the student which part of the stroke needs the most improvement.

Student Directions

The student swims 25 yards of the front crawl four times, attempting to do his personal best each time. During the first trial, the student should focus on having his elbows high. During the next trial, he should focus on reaching forward. During the last two trials, he should focus on high elbow recovery with body roll.

Go! Go! Ghost!

Skill 5.2—Front Crawl for 25 Yards With Rhythmic Breathing, High Elbows, and Body Roll

Equipment

None

Preparation

Make up a story about a ghost.

Formation

The student is in the deep end with 25 yards of clear space in front of her.

Instructor Directions

Explain that you will tell a ghost story. Each time the student hears the word *ghost*, she should put her face in the water and swim with high elbows and body roll as fast as she can away from the ghost. After 10 strokes, she treads water and listens (10 seconds or less) to the next part of the story, waiting for the next time you say the word *ghost*. The activity is over when she has swum 25 yards.

Student Directions

The student swims the front crawl for 10 arm strokes with high elbows and body roll after hearing the word *ghost*. When she has completed 10 strokes, she treads water to listen to more of the ghost story and repeats the 10 strokes whenever she hears the word *ghost*. She repeats this sequence until she has swum 25 yards.

Backstroke

The backstroke is the fastest way to swim on your back. Students need to be careful when using this stroke because, unlike with other strokes, they cannot see where they are going. The backstroke starts from a push off the wall—on the back with the ears in the water, the body straight and mostly horizontal, and the arms either at the sides or above the head. The arms move in opposition with the thumbs coming out of the water first and the pinkies entering the water first. The body rolls slightly toward the arm entering the water, followed by bending the arm, catching water, and pushing water toward the feet. A flutter kick happens throughout the stroke. Whereas the backstroke uses a flutter kick and alternate arms motion, the elementary backstroke uses a whip kick and symmetrical underwater arm motions.

Cues

- Ears in the water, look up.
- Keep thumbs up, pinkies in.
- Roll the opposite shoulder to the sky.
- Keep your head still.
- Bend your elbow and cup your hand to catch the water.
- Palm the basketball to push water toward your feet.

Differentiation

- Use physical assistance to hold the student and rotate his body as his pinky reaches back for the water.
- Allow the student to use lightweight fins to assist with the flutter kick while practicing the arm stroke.
- Have the student use a flotation belt around the waist.
- Provide tactile modeling for students who cannot see a demonstration.
- Give additional cues to students who might need cognitive support.
- Give extra demonstrations and be more animated in teaching the part of the stroke you want the student to learn.
- Have the student practice one arm at a time of the arm stroke on land, lying on the bottom seat of the bleacher.

Wind Me Up

Skill 5.3—Backstroke for 12 Yards With Above-the-Water Recovery

Equipment
None

Preparation
None

Formation
The instructor and the student are on the pool deck for the first part of the activity and in the pool in waist- or chest-deep water for the second part of the activity.

Instructor Directions
Pretend to be a windup toy and move your arms backward in opposition as in the backstroke. Then pretend to wind up the student by turning a pretend knob on his back so he can imitate your windup toy arm motions. Have him get into the pool and swim like a windup toy for 12 yards, concentrating on the arms fully coming out the water with each stroke.

Student Directions
Once you have wound up the student on land, he rotates his arms in opposition backward as in the backstroke. In the pool he can use the windup energy to swim 12 yards using the backstroke. This activity is a great motivator, especially with young students who are getting tired or bored.

High Five

Skill 5.3—Backstroke for 12 Yards With Above-the-Water Recovery

Equipment
Backstroke flags; 8 to 10 laminated hand shapes, each suspended by a 5-foot string

Preparation
Create hand shapes and hang them from the backstroke flags within reach of the student as she is doing the backstroke under the flags.

Formation
The student starts in waist- or chest-deep water against the wall of the pool that is parallel to the hanging backstroke flags with the laminated hands dangling from them.

Instructor Directions
Explain to the student that she will be swimming the backstroke across the width of the pool underneath the backstroke flags. As she does the backstroke, her hands should touch the suspended hand shapes for a backward high five.

Student Directions

The student swims widthwise across the pool and tries to get her backstroking arms out of the water to backward high-five the hand shapes hanging from the flags.

Rainbow Backstroke Start

Skill 5.3—Backstroke for 12 Yards With Above-the-Water Recovery

Equipment

None

Preparation

None

Formation

The instructor is standing 12 yards from the wall in at least 5 feet (1.5 m) of water. The student is standing on the instructor's bent legs (thighs) facing the instructor.

Instructor Directions

Explain or demonstrate the backstroke start and say that it's like being a rainbow. Help the student step up onto your bent legs and say "Ready, set, go," which is the signal for the student to perform a backstroke start (i.e., arched back and arms above her head). For safety, monitor the student during the arch entry so she does not go deep into the water. The student then swims 12 yards of the backstroke to the wall.

Student Directions

On your signal, the student gently pushes off your thighs (making a rainbow with her body) and swims the backstroke to the wall.

The swimmer makes a rainbow with her body to learn the backstroke start.

How Straight Can You Swim?

Skill 5.4—Backstroke for 25 Yards With Above-the-Water Recovery

Equipment
Two plastic traffic cones

Preparation
Place one traffic cone on the deck at one end of the pool and another one on the other end to form a straight line.

Formation
Both the student and the instructor are in waist- or chest-deep water at the pool wall in front of one of the traffic cones.

Instructor Directions
Explain that the student will swim the backstroke with her eyes closed and try to stay in a straight line. You will swim next to her to keep her from bumping into the wall or other swimmers. After she has completed 25 yards of the backstroke with her eyes closed, point out where she ended in relation to the start and finish cones. If the student is not swimming straight, it could be because her arms are crossing the midline of her body. If this is the case, explain to her that as her arm enters the water, it should be directly above her shoulder, not crossing the midline of her body.

Student Directions
The student attempts to swim in a straight line for 25 yards with her eyes closed. After receiving your feedback, she attempts to swim a straight line again.

Backstroke Balance

Skill 5.4—Backstroke for 25 Yards With Above-the-Water Recovery

Equipment
One ring toss sets with three to five plastic rings

Preparation
Place plastic rings on the side of the pool where the student will begin and the ring toss stick on the deck 25 yards away.

Formation
The student is at one side of the pool in any depth of water with 25 yards of clear space in front of him.

Instructor Directions
Demonstrate the backstroke for 25 yards while balancing a plastic diving ring on your abdomen or chest. Then ask the student to choose a colored ring and do the same. When he reaches the other side, he is to remove the ring from his abdomen, toss it to a ring toss stick, and swim the backstroke to the start for another ring.

Explain that the goal is to move as many rings as possible and get them onto the ring toss stick. Repeat as many times as desired.

Student Directions

The student balances a plastic ring on his abdomen or chest for 25 yards while doing the backstroke. He then tosses it onto the ring toss stick and swims back to the start to collect another ring, continuing until he has tossed all rings onto the stick.

Moving Cargo 1

Skill 5.4—Backstroke for 25 Yards With Above-the-Water Recovery

Equipment

A variety of motivating and small pieces of equipment that can be balanced on the body or slipped onto the wrist such as lightweight diving rings or diving sticks

Preparation

Arrange the equipment on one end of the pool 25 yards from the student.

Formation

The student is at one side of the pool in any depth of water with a 25-yard clear path in front of her.

Instructor Directions

Explain that the student is to perform the backstroke 25 yards to where the items are and bring them back to her starting place one at a time while maintaining correct form. She does this for five minutes, at which point you count how many items she has moved. If at any point she breaks correct form, the item she is carrying at that time does not count in the total. Observe the student during the activity and give feedback, including cues.

Student Directions

The student swims 25-yard segments and tries to move as many items as she can in five minutes while maintaining correct stroke form.

Elementary Backstroke

In level 4, the student uses any kick with the correct arms stroke while performing the elementary backstroke. In level 5, the student must use the whip kick and a glide.

Cues

- Monkey, airplane, soldier
- Glide
- Feet down, out and around
- Head back with ears in the water
- Glide 1, 2, 3

Differentiation
- Have the student practice the kick while sitting on a chair on the deck before getting into the pool.
- Use physical guidance to move the student's legs through the sequence.
- Use verbal cues: "Monkey, airplane, kick, soldier."

AFAP (As Few As Possible)

Skill 5.5—Elementary Backstroke With Whip Kick for 12 Yards

Equipment
None

Preparation
None

Formation
In any depth of water, the student is holding the wall with two hands and with feet on the wall and head back. He is in the lane closest to the deck, where the instructor will walk to view the student as he swims.

Instructor Directions
Demonstrate the elementary backstroke for 12 yards, and then get out of the pool and walk along the pool deck as the student swims 12 yards of the elementary backstroke, keeping track of how many strokes he takes.

Student Directions
The student swims 12 yards of the pool using the elementary backstroke, attempting to use as few strokes as possible by using strong kicks and strong arm strokes.

Balance Challenge

Skill 5.5—Elementary Backstroke With Whip Kick for 12 Yards

Equipment
Plastic animal or any waterproof object

Preparation
None

Formation
The student is at the wall in the deep end of the pool.

Instructor Directions
Demonstrate doing the elementary backstroke with a small object on your abdomen or chest. Then have the student try swimming this stroke for 12 yards without dropping the object.

Student Directions

The student swims 12 yards of the elementary backstroke with a small object on her abdomen or chest trying to keep it there for the entire swim.

Minus One

Skill 5.6—Elementary Backstroke With Whip Kick for 25 Yards

Equipment
None

Preparation
None

Formation
In any depth of water, the student is holding the wall with two hands and with feet on the wall and head back. The student is in the lane closest to the deck, where the instructor will walk to view the student as he swims.

Instructor Directions
Demonstrate the elementary backstroke and then get out of the pool and walk along and observe as the student swims 25 yards of the elementary backstroke. Keep track of how many strokes he takes.

Student Directions
The student swims 25 yards using the elementary backstroke and attempting to use as few strokes as possible by using strong kicks and strong arm strokes. When he reaches the end and is resting, tell him how many strokes he took. Challenge him to do a second 25-yard swim and try to use one less stroke by making his stroke more efficient.

Happy Birthday Swim

Skill 5.6—Elementary Backstroke With Whip Kick for 25 Yards

Equipment
None

Preparation
None

Formation
The student is at the wall of the pool in any depth of water.

Instructor Directions
Demonstrate the elementary backstroke with an exaggerated glide. Then have the student try it. As she is gliding, sing one line of "Happy Birthday" and then wait until the next glide to sing the next line. The activity ends when the student has completed 25 yards and the song is over.

Student Directions

The student pushes off the wall and starts the elementary backstroke. When she gets to the glide portion of the stroke, she holds the glide as you sing the first line of "Happy Birthday." She continues swimming and extends each glide until you finish a line of the song.

Breaststroke

In level 4, students use breaststroke arms with any kick for 12 yards. In this level, they improve their breaststroke skills by performing the stroke with a whip kick for 12 and then 25 yards.

Cues

- Fast pull (no pause), long slide
- Stretch to breathe
- Chin down
- Kick and undulate

Differentiation

- Break this skill down into smaller parts such as bending the ankles and bringing them to the buttocks.
- Have the student practice the kick on land while lying on a mat with the legs hanging over the water.
- Use physical guidance to move the student's arms through the motions.
- Use colored raised tape on the wall in the shape of an upside-down heart for the student to trace before trying the arm motions in the water.
- Use additional verbal cues that are motivating to the student ("Pointy hands, draw your heart, kick your butt").

Clean Up the Pool 1

Skill 5.7—Breaststroke With Whip Kick for 12 Yards

Equipment

Pool noodles cut into 6-inch (15 cm) pieces (at least 10 pieces per student)

Preparation

Scatter floating pool noodle pieces throughout the pool.

Formation

The student is at the wall of the pool in waist- or chest-deep water facing the floating noodle pieces.

Instructor Directions

Demonstrate performing the breaststroke toward one of the noodle pieces, retrieve it, and bring it to the deck. Tell the student that the pool is messy and needs to be cleaned, but he must use only the breaststroke to reach the objects. Remind the student that he needs to swim at least 12 yards.

Student Directions

The student performs the breaststroke to get to the floating noodle pieces, collects them one at a time, and brings them back to the wall to clean up the pool.

Pay the Toll

Skill 5.8—Breaststroke With Whip Kick for 25 Yards

Equipment

Two pool noodles, a traffic cone with a laminated sign saying *Finish Line* taped to it

Preparation

Laminate a sign that says *Finish Line* and tape it to a traffic cone. Place the cone 25 yards from the student (on the other end of the pool).

Formation

The instructor holds two pool noodles in the shape of an X in front of the student, who is in waist- or chest-deep water holding on to the wall with one hand and with one foot on the wall.

Instructor Directions

Hold the pool noodles in the shape of an X in front of the student and say "Take your mark, Go" as you lift the tollgate up. The student swims the breaststroke to the finish line 25 yards away. When he touches the finish line wall, he has to pay the gatekeeper's toll. The instructor walks to the other side to collect the payment. (The payment is a high five.)

Student Directions

The student pushes off the wall and swims the breaststroke to the finish line 25 yards away, where he gives you a high five.

Treading

In level 3, students treaded water for 10 seconds in chin-deep water. In level 4, they treaded water for one minute. In this level, students tread water for at least two minutes.

Dance Dance

Skill 5.9—Tread in at Least 9 Feet (2.7 m) of Water for Two Minutes

Equipment

Music (age and language appropriate), floating pool mat or pool noodles

Treading can be fun when set to music.

Preparation

Set up a sound system and cue up age- and language-appropriate music. Have a way to turn the music on and off (e.g., a remote).

Formation

The student is in the deep end of the pool (at least 9 ft, or 2.7 m, deep), and the instructor is sitting on the edge of the pool.

Instructor Directions

Explain that in this activity, dancing to music involves treading water. Demonstrate treading water while music is playing for at least one minute. Then have someone turn it off while you rest on a mat or over a pool noodle. Then have the student tread water while you play music for two minutes and rest on a mat or pool noodle when you turn the music off.

Student Directions

The student dances (i.e., treads water) for two minutes while the music is playing, rests for 30 seconds on a floating mat or pool noodle, and then treads water for another minute when the music starts again. This goes on for the duration of one song (about four minutes).

Water Polo

Skill 5.9—Tread in at Least 9 Feet (2.7 m) of Water for Two Minutes

Equipment

One beach ball, water polo goals or two sets of two cones with a string across them to create a goal

Preparation

This activity requires at least two students. Set two goals on the pool deck in the deep end.

Formation

Students are in two teams in the deep end of the pool.

Instructor Directions

Demonstrate treading water and shooting a beach ball at a goal on the pool deck. Tell the students to tread water and attempt to score a goal by shooting the ball at the net.

Student Directions

The students play a modified version of traditional water polo with the focus on properly treading water and building their endurance to tread for a longer time. They attempt to shoot the beach ball to score on their opponent's goal while treading water.

Two Minutes to Win It

Skill 5.9—Tread in at Least 9 Feet (2.7 m) of Water for Two Minutes

Equipment

Hula hoop, 10 to 20 small beach balls

Preparation

Float a hula hoop in deep water and scatter 10 to 20 small beach balls around the deep end area within 20 feet (6 m) of the hoop.

Formation

The student and the instructor are treading water around a hula hoop, with at least 10 small beach balls floating nearby in the deep end of the pool.

Instructor Directions

Demonstrate treading water and reaching for beach balls to toss into the floating hula hoop. Then say "Go" and keep time (two minutes per game) to determine how many balls the student can toss into the hoop in two minutes.

Student Directions

The student throws as many balls as he can into the hula hoop in two minutes, while treading water.

Water Volleyball

Skill 5.9—Tread in at Least 9 Feet (2.7 m) of Water for Two Minutes

Equipment

Beach ball, swimming lane line that separates competitive swim lanes

Preparation

Make sure the lane line is in place in the deep end.

Formation

The student is treading water on one side of the lane line, and the instructor is on the other side, also treading water, in the deep end.

Instructor Directions

Gently strike the beach ball into the air over the lane line toward the student, who is treading water. The student strikes the ball back to you for a fun game of beach water volleyball. Playing games that require students to remain in relatively the same spot in deep water forces them to use treading skills without actively focusing on how long they are treading. Provide rest breaks as needed.

Student Directions

The student volleys a beach ball back and forth over a lane line with you while treading water in the deep end.

Sidestroke

In level 4, students performed the arm motion of the sidestroke with any kick for 12 yards. In this level, students perform the sidestroke with the scissors kick.

12-Yard Sidestroke Switch

Skill 5.10—Sidestroke for 12 Yards Using the Scissors Kick

Equipment

Small ball or object that fits easily in the student's hand

Preparation

None

Formation

The student is on her side perpendicular to the wall, with her head and lead hand pointing in the direction of the opposite pool wall, and the trailing hand holding the wall near her feet. In her lead hand she holds a small ball or object.

Instructor Directions

Demonstrate the glide off the side, and show how to transfer the ball from the lead hand to the top hand, and then, on the next stroke, from the top hand to the lead (bottom) hand to practice the coordination of the arms during the sidestroke for 12 yards. Have the student switch the object from hand to hand while swimming the sidestroke using the scissors kick. Provide encouragement and feedback when necessary.

Student Directions

The student swims the sidestroke with a scissors kick, transferring the ball from hand to hand on each stroke. Having an object to manipulate gives students a sense of what their bodies should be doing throughout the stroke and helps them coordinate the movement of the arms coming together and then separating.

Towboat

Skill 5.11—Sidestroke for 25 Yards Using the Scissors Kick

Equipment

Lifeguard floating rescue tube, waterproof animal toy

Preparation

Find a lifeguard rescue tube (buoy) that is not being used by the guards, and have a waterproof animal toy on hand.

Formation

The student has the strap of the rescue tube across his shoulder in the shallow end of the pool with 25 yards of clear space in front of him. The instructor places a waterproof animal on the rescue tube. (A rubber band may be needed to secure it to the tube.)

Instructor Directions

Demonstrate how to put the rescue tube over your shoulder and perform the sidestroke while towing the rescue tube with the animal on it behind you (do not hold it, just let it follow). Then encourage the student to do the same, and provide stroke feedback when necessary.

Student Directions

The student swims the sidestroke using the scissors kick for 25 yards while towing an animal on a rescue tube slung over the shoulder of the bottom, or lead, arm.

How Many Apples?

Skill 5.11—Sidestroke for 25 Yards Using the Scissors Kick

Equipment

None

Preparation

None

Formation

The student is at the wall in chest-deep water.

Instructor Directions

Explain the cues of the sidestroke: *pick the apple, put it in the basket, kick*. Then demonstrate the stroke and have the student swim one length of the pool (25 yards). Record the number of strokes and provide feedback to try to decrease the number of strokes at the next session.

Student Directions

The student swims the sidestroke using the scissor kick for 25 yards, keeping track of the number of strokes she takes (i.e., apples she picked). She will try to decrease the number of strokes at the next session based on instructor feedback.

LEVEL

6

Longer-Distance and Competitive Swimming

Modified Texas Woman's University
Aquatic Assessment: Level 6

Student's name: _____ Instructor's name: _____

Student's date of birth: _____   Date: _____

Page number	Skill number	Skill description	Yes	No	Comments
177	6.1	Front crawl 50 yards			
178	6.2	Front crawl 100 yards			
180	6.3	Backstroke 50 yards			
181	6.4	Backstroke 100 yards			
182	6.5	Breaststroke 50 yards with coordinated arms, legs, and breathing			
183	6.6	Sidestroke 50 yards			
185	6.7	Sidestroke 100 yards			
188	6.8	Perform an open turn on front			
191	6.9	Perform a flip turn from a front crawl			
192	6.10	Front crawl 50 yards using a flip turn at 25 yards			
195	6.11	Breaststroke 50 yards using a legal turn at 25 yards			
197	6.12	Backstroke 50 yards using a backstroke flip turn at 25 yards			
199	6.13	Perform the butterfly stroke progression 10 times			
200	6.14	Butterfly with fins 12 yards			
201	6.15	Butterfly 25 yards			
202	6.16	Swim the individual medley 100 yards			

General comments:

Modified from Texas Woman's University Aquatic Assessment.

From M. Lepore, L. Columna, and L. Friedlander Litzner, 2015, *Assessments and activities for teaching swimming* (Champaign, IL: Human Kinetics).

L evel 6 includes most of the skills students are expected to master to successfully and safely participate in aquatic environments. Most students who reach level 6 are able to participate in basic competitive swimming events and have the baseline swim skills needed for taking part in more advanced aquatic activities such as water polo, synchronized swimming, and calm-water aquatic adventures. This level emphasizes longer-distance swimming, flip turns, and performing strokes for competitive swimming or pre-lifeguard training. Activities for this level take place in deep water.

Front Crawl

In level 5, students performed the front crawl for 25 yards with good form. In this level, they do the same, but for longer distances. For additional description, cues, and differentiation, see level 4.

Math Time

Skill 6.1—Front Crawl 50 Yards

Equipment
Stopwatch

Preparation
None

Formation
The student is in the pool, holding the wall with one hand.

Instructor Directions
Explain to the student that she will swim 50 yards of the front crawl and count every time her arm comes out of the water, while you will keep track of how long it takes her to swim the 50 yards. Explain that she should move as fast as possible, using as few strokes as possible. When finished, have her calculate her time per stroke by dividing the number of seconds it took her to swim the 50 yards by the number of strokes she took. Ask her to swim the 50 yards again and decrease the time and the number of strokes.

Student Directions
The student will swim 50 yards of the front crawl and count every time her arm comes out of the water, while trying to swim as fast as possible. You will keep track of how long it takes her to swim the 50 yards. When finished, she will calculate her time per stroke by dividing the number of seconds it took her to swim the 50 yards by the number of strokes she took. She will swim the 50 yards again and try to decrease the time and the number of strokes.

Breathe Much?

Skill 6.1—Front Crawl 50 Yards

Equipment
None

Preparation
None

Formation
The student is at the pool wall.

Instructor Directions
Demonstrate breathing every other stroke and then ask the student to do the same. As a safety precaution, pay close attention to the student to make sure she does not get lightheaded from breathing only every other stroke.

Student Directions
The student swims the front crawl for 50 yards, attempting to breathe every other stroke. (One stroke equals two arm pulls.)

In a Heartbeat

Skill 6.2—Front Crawl 100 Yards

Equipment
Clock or stopwatch, whiteboard with dry erase markers, calculator

Preparation
Teach the student to obtain his heart rate either on his wrist or on the side of his neck by counting his heartbeats for periods of 15, 20, or 60 seconds. Research how to find one's heart rate. The website of the American Heart Association provides information on how to calculate target heart rates. For additional information, you can visit www.heart.org/HEARTORG/GettingHealthy/PhysicalActivity/FitnessBasics/Target-Heart-Rates_UCM_434341_Article.jsp.

Formation
The student is at the pool wall.

Instructor Directions
Explain why reaching a target heart rate is critical for improving cardiorespiratory endurance, and how to calculate one's target heart rate using a whiteboard or calculator. Demonstrate finding the heart rate quickly using the fingertips on the neck or wrist. Have the student find his heartbeat, count it for 6 seconds, and multiply the number of beats by 10. Then help the student determine his target training zone.

Student Directions

The student calculates his target heart rate and then swims the front crawl for 100 yards, attempting to reach his target heart rate zone. He repeats the swim as many times as his fitness level allows, in an attempt to reach his target zone.

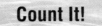

Count It!

Skill 6.2—Front Crawl 100 Yards

Equipment

None

Preparation

Have on hand, from a previous lesson or activity, the number of strokes it typically takes the student to swim the front crawl 25 yards.

Formation

The student is at the pool wall.

Instructor Directions

Tell the student the number of strokes she usually takes to swim the front crawl 25 yards. Encourage the student to match her number of strokes or to decrease the number of strokes.

Student Directions

The student swims 100 yards trying to use only the number of strokes she normally takes, or fewer, for each 25-yard segment.

Beat the Clock

Skill 6.2—Front Crawl 100 Yards

Equipment

Submersible equipment that is motivating to the student, stopwatch

Preparation

Scatter equipment underwater at the wall at each end of the pool.

Formation

The student is at the pool wall.

Instructor Directions

Explain that the objective of this activity is to swim at least 100 yards by swimming certain distances in a set amount of time (e.g., 25 yards in 50 seconds). Use a stopwatch to keep time. Each time the student beats the clock, he picks up a submerged object and puts it on the pool deck. At the end of the activity, count the number of objects on the pool deck and compare it to the number of times the student swam a length. Tell the student the percentage of his success in meeting the objective.

Student Directions

The student swims the front crawl for a specific distance and attempts to beat the time you have set (based on an assessment of his skill). If he reaches the end of the length under the time set, he picks up a submerged object and places it on the pool deck. Picking up a submerged object gives the student a sense of purpose, a way to count successful laps, and a short break if he lacks endurance.

Backstroke

In level 5, students swim for a maximum of 25 yards; now the distance is increased to 50 and 100 yards. For additional description, cues, and differentiation, see level 4 and figure L4.3.

Poker Chip Challenge

Skill 6.3—Backstroke 50 Yards

Equipment

Several poker chips per swimmer

Preparation

None

Formation

The student is holding and facing the wall.

Instructor Directions

Demonstrate doing the backstroke while balancing a poker chip on your forehead. Tell the student to swim 50 yards without dropping the poker chip.

Student Directions

The student swims 50 yards of the backstroke with a poker chip balanced on her forehead, trying not to drop the chip. If she drops the chip, she should come back to the start to get another one and begin again.

High Five Fifty

Skill 6.3—Backstroke 50 Yards

Equipment

Backstroke flags; 8 to 10 laminated hand shapes, each suspended by a 5-foot string

Preparation

Create hand shapes and hang them from the backstroke flags. Measure how far they hang to be sure the student can reach them as he is doing the backstroke.

Formation

The student is against the wall of the pool that is parallel to the hanging backstroke flags and hands.

Instructor Directions

Explain to the student that he will be swimming the backstroke across the width of the pool underneath the backstroke flags. As he does the backstroke, swimming the equivalent of 50 yards, his hands should touch the suspended hand shapes for backward high fives.

Student Directions

The student swims widthwise across the pool, swimming the equivalent of 50 yards while trying to get his backstroking arms out of the water to backward high-five the hand shapes hanging from the flags.

Clean Up the Pool 2

Skill 6.4—Backstroke 100 Yards

Equipment

Pool noodle cut into 6-inch (15 cm) pieces (at least 10 pieces per student) with laminated backstroke skills adhered to them (e.g., backstroke 25 yards, flutter kick on back 50 yards)

Preparation

Scatter the noodle pieces throughout the pool.

Formation

The student is at the pool wall.

Instructor Directions

Explain that the student will swim the backstroke until she bumps into a noodle piece. At that point she reads it, tosses it on the deck in a designated area, and performs the task written on it. She does this until there are no more noodle pieces to encounter. All tasks should involve the backstroke.

Student Directions

The student backstrokes until she bumps into a noodle piece, at which point she stops, reads what is on the noodle piece, tosses it to the deck, and performs the skill. She must swim the equivalent of 100 yards before this activity is complete.

Moving Cargo 2

Skill 6.4—Backstroke 100 Yards

Equipment

A variety of small, motivating pieces of equipment that can be balanced on the body or slipped onto the wrist

Preparation

Arrange the equipment at end of the pool deck, 25 yards from the student.

Formation

After demonstrating, the instructor goes to the deck to observe the student performing the backstroke. The student is at one side of the pool with a clear 25-yard path in front of him.

Instructor Directions

Demonstrate swimming the backstroke for 25 yards using correct stroke form. Then ask the student to swim four segments of 25 yards and move as many items (as fast as possible) from one end of the pool to the other by balancing them on his body or wearing them on his wrist.

Student Directions

The student performs the backstroke in four 25-yard segments and moves as many items (as fast as possible) across the pool as possible while maintaining correct stroke form. If he breaks correct form, his cargo for that run is not counted in the final count of items moved.

Breaststroke

In level 5, students performed the breaststroke for a distance of 25 yards using a whip kick. In this level, they swim the breaststroke for 50 yards using coordinated arms, legs (whip kick), and breathing. For additional description, cues, and differentiation, see level 5.

Count My Strokes!

Skill 6.5—Breaststroke 50 Yards With Coordinated Arms, Legs, and Breathing

Equipment

None

Preparation

None

Formation

The student is at the wall of the pool.

Instructor Directions

To help the student achieve her most efficient stroke count, count how many strokes she takes in a 50-yard swim of the breaststroke. After she has completed the trial, provide encouragement and feedback to help her decrease the number of strokes in a subsequent swim.

Student Directions

The student swims the breaststroke for 50 yards while you count the number of strokes she takes. After receiving your feedback, she redoes the swim, aiming to reach a lower stroke count by being more powerful, more streamlined, and more efficient in each stroke.

Video Me

Skill 6.5—Breaststroke 50 Yards With Coordinated Arms, Legs, and Breathing

Equipment
Video device

Preparation
Use a video device to record the student's performance. For accuracy, you may want to use a tripod.

Formation
The student is at the wall of the pool.

Instructor Directions
After getting permission from the student's guardian or parent (if appropriate), videorecord the student doing the breaststroke. Then watch the recording with the student, counting how many seconds he glides during each stroke. After this review, give him some feedback for increasing his glide time.

Student Directions
The student completes two lengths (or the equivalent of 50 yards) of the breaststroke. He then reviews a video of his swim and, after receiving some tips from you, attempts to glide longer in the next trial.

Sidestroke

In level 5, the distance to perform the sidestroke is 25 yards. In level 6, students are challenged to perform the sidestroke for at least 100 yards using good form.

Save the Wildlife

Skill 6.6—Sidestroke 50 Yards

Equipment
Lifeguard floating rescue tube, small waterproof toy animal no bigger than 4 inches (10 cm) tall

Preparation
Find a lifeguard rescue tube (buoy) that is not being used by the guards, and have a waterproof animal toy on hand.

Formation
The instructor, standing beside the student, places the waterproof animal toy onto the rescue tube. (A rubber band or tie may be needed to secure the animal to the tube.)

Instructor Directions

Demonstrate how to put the rescue tube over one shoulder and perform the sidestroke with that arm while towing the rescue tube with the animal on it behind you (not holding it, just letting it follow). Encourage the student and provide stroke feedback when necessary.

Student Directions

The student swims the sidestroke for two 25-yard lengths while towing a waterproof animal or other toy on a rescue tube that is slung over the shoulder of the bottom, or lead, arm.

Junior Lifesaver

Skill 6.6—Sidestroke 50 Yards

Equipment

Lifeguard rescue buoy

Preparation

None

Formation

Students are in pairs in the water.

Instructor Directions

Explain that this activity gets students ready for pre-lifeguard training, and it does *not* mean that they are lifeguards! Demonstrate towing a person on a rescue tube by using the sidestroke with only the lead (bottom) arm moving and the trail arm (top) holding the rescue tube. Then have students practice this in pairs. Supervise this activity carefully, discourage fooling around, encourage students, and give feedback when appropriate.

Student Directions

Students are in pairs. One student places the strap of the lifeguard rescue tube over her head and on the opposite shoulder and does the sidestroke, while her partner holds the buoy. She then tows her partner on the buoy using the sidestroke with only the bottom arm moving. The students then switch roles.

The sidestroke is an important skill when learning lifeguarding techniques.

How Many Apples in 50 Yards

Skill 6.6—Sidestroke 50 Yards

Equipment
None

Preparation
None

Formation
The student is at the wall of the pool.

Instructor Directions
Explain the cues of the sidestroke (*pick the apple, put it in the basket, kick*). Then demonstrate the stroke and have the student swim two lengths of the pool—50 yards. Record the number of strokes and provide feedback to try to decrease the number of strokes at the next session.

Student Directions
The student swims the sidestroke using the scissor kick for 50 yards, keeping track of the number of strokes she takes (i.e., apples she picked). The student will try to decrease the number of strokes at the next session based on instructor feedback.

Clean Up the Pool 3

Skill 6.7—Sidestroke 100 Yards

Equipment
Pool noodles cut into 6-inch (15 cm) pieces (at least five pieces per students) with sidestroke skills laminated and adhered to them

Preparation
Cut pool noodles into 6-inch pieces. Write sidestroke skills on five different index cards, laminate the index cards, and adhere them to five noodle pieces. Scatter the noodle pieces throughout 25 yards of the pool.

Formation
The student is at the wall of the pool.

Instructor Directions
Tell the student to swim the sidestroke 100 yards; when he bumps into a noodle piece, he is to tread water, read the skill, toss the pool noodle to the edge of the pool, and perform the skill. Ideas for skills include scissor kick only for 5 yards, arm stroke only for 10 yards, reverse sides.

Student Directions
The student swims the sidestroke 100 yards; when he sees a floating noodle piece, he treads water, reads the skill, tosses the pool noodle to the edge of the pool, and performs the skill presented on the pool noodle.

100-Yard Sidestroke Switch

Skill 6.7—Sidestroke 100 Yards

Equipment
Small ball that fits easily in the student's hand

Preparation
None

Formation
The student is on her side perpendicular to the wall, with her head and lead hand pointing in the direction of the opposite pool wall, and the trailing hand holding the wall near her feet. In her lead hand she holds a small ball or object.

Instructor Directions
Demonstrate the glide off the side, and show how to transfer the ball from the lead hand to the top hand. On the next stroke, transfer the ball from the top hand to the lead (bottom) hand. Explain that this will help the student practice coordinating her arms while swimming 100 yards of the sidestroke. Provide encouragement and feedback when necessary.

Student Directions
The student swims the sidestroke 100 yards, transferring the ball from hand to hand with each stroke. The ball gives the student a sense of what her body should be doing throughout the stroke and helps her practice bringing her arms together and then separating them in a coordinated way.

Open Turn on the Front for the Front Crawl

An open turn (see figure L6.1) is used to turn at the wall when swimming laps in a pool; it is for those who cannot perform, or have not yet learned, the flip turn. An open turn begins with the lead hand touching or grabbing the wall; the elbow bends as the body curls up, and the head comes up quickly to take a breath as the feet are planted on the wall facing away from the lead arm. The trailing arm remains behind the body, and the face goes back into the water as the arm holding the wall moves in an arc to meet the extended arm and the swimmer pushes off in a streamlined position away from the wall. The entire body is submerged to complete the open turn (American Red Cross, 2009).

Cues
- Touch the wall with one hand; the other hand trails.
- Fold into the wall; don't pull into it.
- Bring only the head out of the water to breathe.
- Push away and exhale.
- Stay horizontal and low (underwater).
- Streamline yourself under the water.

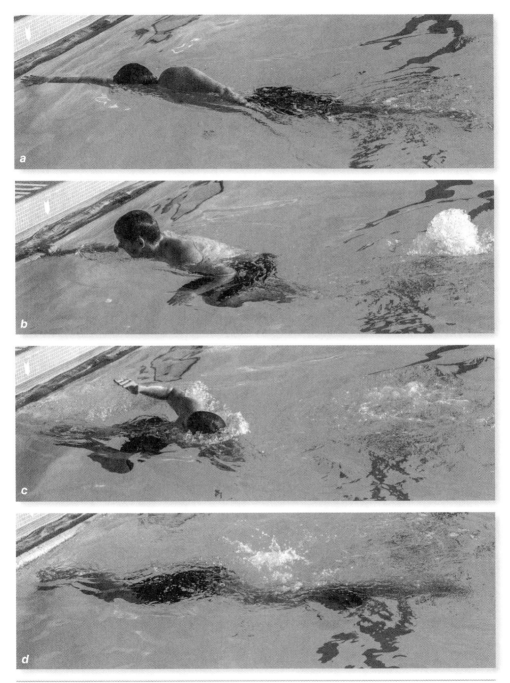

Figure L6.1 The open turn on front starts by *(a)* coming into the wall with only one hand, followed by *(b)* the body curling in and up so that *(c)* the feet can plant against the wall to push off as the face returns to the water and the arm that was holding the wall moves in an arc until finally *(d)* the entire body is submerged and streaming away from the wall.

Differentiation

- Provide a hands-on learning session.
- Have the student practice on the deck on a low gym scooter first.
- Give additional verbal cues for each part of the turn.

Reaction Battle Time

Skill 6.8—Perform an Open Turn on Front

Equipment

None

Preparation

None

Formation

The student and instructor are standing side by side in chest-deep water, facing the pool wall 3 yards away.

Instructor Directions

When you say "Go," the student performs the front crawl for 3 yards and performs an open turn at the wall to swim back to you. Tell the student to try to do this in 10 seconds or less. Count out loud.

Student Directions

The student performs the front crawl when you say "Go," completes an open turn at the wall, and returns to you in less than 10 seconds.

Mini Race

Skill 6.8—Perform an Open Turn on Front

Equipment

A traffic cone

Preparation

Place the traffic cone 5 yards from the wall underwater.

Formation

The student is standing next to the instructor at the cone facing the wall.

Instructor Directions

Make believe the student is starting a race and has to go fast to the wall and back to the cone. Demonstrate the front crawl to the wall with an open turn and swim back to the 5-yard mark. Then have the student do it when you say "Go," and watch so you can provide feedback.

Student Directions

The student listens for your cue to swim in, completes an open turn, and swims back to the 5-yard mark.

Need for Speed

Skill 6.8—Perform an Open Turn on Front

Equipment

None

Preparation

None

Formation

The student is at the side of the pool facing across the width of the pool.

Instructor Directions

Tell the student to swim the front crawl the width of the pool as many times as he can in a certain number of minutes. Watch as the student performs a series of open turns while swimming back and forth across the width of the pool. (Swimming the width of the pool increases the number of turns.) Provide feedback when necessary. Set an appropriate amount of time to complete a certain number of laps based on the student's endurance level. If the student begins to feel dizzy, discontinue the activity.

Student Directions

The student attempts to complete as many open turns as he can within a time frame you have established (e.g., three minutes) while swimming the width of the pool. He should strive to use the correct form and follow the cues.

Front Crawl Flip Turn

The flip turn on the front from the front crawl (see figure L6.2) takes determination to learn and coordination to master. The swimmer comes into the wall looking at the T on the bottom or the side of the pool. The hands are by the hips as the head glides toward the wall. The hands are pressed down at the sides, the chin is tucked, and the swimmer blows bubbles from the mouth and nose while somersaulting, planting the feet on the wall, and pushing off toward the other end in a streamlined position. The swimmer turns back onto the front sometime after the push-off. The flip turn is an efficient and fast way to do a continuous swim, but it takes a lot of practice to master.

Cues

- Use your momentum into the wall.
- Keep your hands by your sides.
- Tuck your chin and curl into a ball.
- Flip your legs over and plant your feet on the wall.

- Streamline away from the wall.
- Twist your body back onto your front.

Differentiation

- Break this skill down into very simple parts, and have the student practice only one at a time.
- Use backward chaining (i.e., beginning at the end of the skill and working your way toward the beginning).
- Use a doll with segmented arms and legs to let the student feel the movement of the limbs.
- Have someone provide voice-overs during your demonstrations.

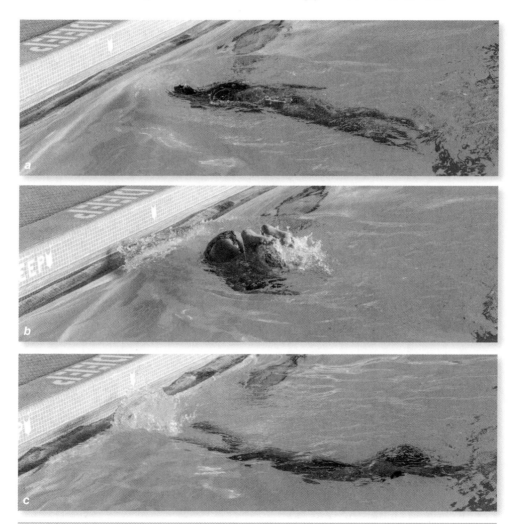

Figure L6.2 As the swimmer comes into the wall for a flip turn, she *(a)* keeps her hands by her side, *(b)* performs the somersault, and *(c)* plants her feet on the wall and pushes off.

- Provide a tapper (i.e., someone who taps the student's shoulder with a pool noodle to designate when to flip).
- Put a kickboard or mat over the gutter to keep the student's feet from hitting the wall and getting hurt.

Biggest Splash

Skill 6.9—Perform a Flip Turn From a Front Crawl

Equipment
None

Preparation
None

Formation
The student is treading water 5 yards from the wall in the deep end, facing the wall. The instructor is sitting on the pool deck, after she does a demonstration.

Instructor Directions
Demonstrate swimming three to five strokes of the front crawl toward the pool wall and perform a flip turn. Emphasize flipping the lower part of the legs over the water and splashing the water before planting the feet on the wall for the flip turn. Then cue the student to do the same. Observe and, when necessary, provide feedback.

Student Directions
The student performs three to five strokes of the front crawl toward the wall and performs a flip turn.

Race Yourself

Skill 6.9—Perform a Flip Turn From a Front Crawl

Equipment
Traffic cone

Preparation
Place a cone in the water 15 yards away from the wall of the pool.

Formation
The student is 15 yards from the wall in chest-deep water, facing the wall. The instructor is on the deck, above where the turn will be performed.

Instructor Directions
Cue the student to start swimming the front crawl, perform a flip turn, and swim back to the cone. Time the student from when she starts and when she returns to the cone.

Student Directions

On your signal, the student swims the front crawl, completes a flip turn, and swims back to the 15-yard mark (the cone). The student competes against herself on each trial, trying to beat her record from her previous trials.

Olympic Gymnast

Skill 6.9—Perform a Flip Turn From a Front Crawl

Equipment

Thin plastic broom stick

Preparation

None

Formation

The student is at the wall 10 yards from the instructor, who is holding the plastic broom stick in chest-deep water.

Instructor Directions

Demonstrate a flip turn (not near the wall) over a plastic broom stick that the student is holding. Explain that the student is to swim 10 yards using the front crawl and will flip turn over the plastic stick like an Olympic gymnast on the bars.

Student Directions

The student will swim using the front crawl toward a plastic broom stick held underwater by you. When he reaches the plastic stick, he will perform a flip turn over the stick in open water and get feedback from you to improve his next try.

Final Countdown

Skill 6.10—Front Crawl 50 Yards Using a Flip Turn at 25 Yards

Equipment

Clock or stopwatch

Preparation

None

Formation

The student is in the deep end of the pool.

Instructor Directions

Explain to the student that you will count down from 60 seconds. She will start to swim at the number of seconds she believes it will take her to swim to 25 yards and back (e.g., 30 seconds). She is to swim the 25 yards, make a flip turn, and swim back. If she gets back just as you reach zero, she wins!

Student Directions

As you count down from 60, the student waits until you get to a number she believes is the time she will need to swim 50 yards with a flip turn and then performs a streamline off the wall. She swims the front crawl 25 yards, does a flip turn at the wall, and swims back.

Raise the Flags

Skill 6.10—Front Crawl 50 Yards Using a Flip Turn at 25 Yards

Equipment

One pair of colorful socks

Preparation

The instructor will provide knee socks that will look like your favorite country flag. The student will put the socks on before getting in the pool.

Formation

The student is in the deep end of the pool holding the wall with one hand.

Instructor Directions

Explain that the student is going to swim the front crawl 25 yards to the end of the pool, do a flip, and swim 25 yards back with a pair of knee socks on. When performing the flip turn, she should exaggerate the lower legs coming out of the water like she is raising the flag.

Student Directions

The student puts on a pair of knee socks that look like a flag, swims the front crawl 25 yards to the end of the pool, does a flip turn (with exaggerated lower-leg action coming out of the water), and swims 25 yards back.

Breaststroke Legal Turn

During the turn for the breaststroke (see figure L6.3), the swimmer must reach out to touch the wall with both hands at once, in the same plane, while on his front. Once a touch has been made, the swimmer drops one shoulder and arm underwater, toward one side, dips the head under as the legs come under the body, and makes contact on the wall with the feet. Then, the swimmer brings the arm that is still in contact with the wall up and over the top of the water to meet the other hand, totally submerges himself and pushes off the wall in a streamlined position at least a foot underwater. As the glide begins to slow down, the swimmer makes a large arm pull with both arms at the same time underwater so the hands end up near the hips. Bringing the hands together near the abdomen and extending them back into the streamlined position as the legs do a breaststroke kick brings the student to the surface to begin the breaststroke again. A butterfly undulation (body waves) and kick are allowed.

Figure L6.3 A breaststroke legal turn *(a)* starts with both hands reaching out to touch the wall, followed by *(b)* dropping one shoulder and arm underwater before *(c)* bringing the remaining arm from the wall and swinging it in an arc into the water in order to turn and *(d)* be positioned back underwater.

Cues

- Two hands touch
- Drop one shoulder
- Feet flat on wall
- Quick breath
- Dip under
- Streamline

Differentiation

- Give additional cues for each part of the turn.
- Provide physical guidance.
- Provide verbal cues.
- Walk through the steps on the deck first.

Tennis Ball Challenge

Skill 6.11—Breaststroke 50 Yards Using a Legal Turn at 25 Yards

Equipment

Tennis ball or pool noodle

Preparation

Give the student a tennis ball or pool noodle.

Formation

The student is in the pool holding a tennis ball under his chin.

Instructor Directions

Demonstrate the breaststroke turn, and then explain that the student is going to swim 50 yards of the breaststroke with a tennis ball (or pool noodle) under his chin. If he loses the ball or noodle, instruct him to put it back under his chin. After he completes the turn, provide feedback about his performance.

Student Directions

The student swims 50 yards of the breaststroke with a tennis ball (or pool noodle) under his chin and tries not to lose the ball (or noodle).

Go Fish

Skill 6.11—Breaststroke 50 Yards Using a Legal Turn at 25 Yards

Equipment

Waterproof playing cards

Preparation

Learn the game Go Fish before this activity. Laminate a deck of plying cards and gather at least two people for this game.

Formation

The students are at the wall in any depth of water.

Instructor Directions

Explain that the students are going to play the game Go Fish, only with a twist. Every time someone says "Go fish," all students must swim the breaststroke 50 yards, making sure to do a legal breaststroke turn at the 25-yard wall. Then deal the cards to the students to begin the game again. Supervise the students and provide corrective feedback as needed.

Student Directions

The students play Go Fish and swim a 50-yard breaststroke each time a player says "Go fish." All students must do a legal breaststroke turn at the 25-yard wall.

Backstroke Flip Turn

In competitive swim meets, swimmers who are completing lengths of the backstroke perform faster with a backstroke flip turn at the wall. The backstroke flip turn is the same as the front flip turn except that at a predetermined distance from the wall (gauged individually by each swimmer in reference to strokes past the backstroke flags), the swimmer flips onto the abdomen and performs the front flip turn. As the swimmer pushes off the wall, he remains on his back to glide underwater and then gradually surfaces to continue the backstroke.

Cues

- Count your strokes past the flags.
- Look for the color change on the lane lines.
- Roll over to your front.
- Keep both hands at your sides.
- Use your momentum into the wall.
- Keep your hands by your side.
- Tuck your chin and curl into a ball.
- Flip your legs over and plant your feet on the wall.
- Streamline away from the wall.

Differentiation

- Break this skill down into very simple parts and have the student practice only one part at a time.
- Use backward chaining (i.e., beginning at the end of the skill and working your way backward to the beginning).
- Use a doll with segmented arms and legs to let student feel the movement of the limbs.
- Have someone provide voice-overs during your demonstrations.

- Provide a tapper (i.e., someone who taps the student's shoulder with a pool noodle to designate when to flip).
- Put a kickboard or mat over the gutter to keep the student's feet from hitting the wall and getting hurt.

11 and 1

Skill 6.12—Backstroke 50 Yards Using a Backstroke Flip Turn at 25 Yards

Equipment
Waterproof video camera

Preparation
Be sure the video camera is charged and ready to use.

Formation
The student is at the pool wall.

Instructor Directions
Record the student doing the backstroke for 50 yards, and then review the recording with her.

Student Directions
The student swims 50 yards of the backstroke. Afterward, she reviews your recording to see whether her arms entered the water at the 11 and 1 o'clock positions (on a clock). After reviewing the tape, the student reattempts the trial, making adjustments to her arm motions. After the second trial, she reviews the recording to examine her flip turn.

Log Roll

Skill 6.12—Backstroke 50 Yards Using a Backstroke Flip Turn at 25 Yards

Equipment
None

Preparation
None

Formation
The student is in the lane closest to the side of the pool. The instructor walks along the deck following the student as he swims.

Instructor Directions
Demonstrate swimming the backstroke for 25 yards, performing the rollover and front flip turn, and swimming the backstroke 25 yards back to the start. Explain that he will do the same and that you will yell "Log roll" to alert him that it is time to roll over onto his front and perform the front flip turn.

Student Directions

The student swims 25 yards of the backstroke, and when you yell "Log roll," he rolls over onto his front and performs the front flip turn. Once he has completed the turn, he swims the backstroke 25 yards back to the starting point.

Butterfly

The butterfly is said to be the most difficult stroke because it requires a lot of strength and impeccable coordination and timing. Both arms come out of the water at the same time and then move underneath the body simultaneously (see figure L6.4). The kick for the butterfly is the dolphin kick in which the legs stay together as the body performs a wavelike (undulating) motion.

Figure L6.4 The butterfly stroke uses *(a)* an underwater arm pull that resembles a key hole with *(b)* two dolphin kicks, and *(c)* the arms come out of the water at the same time.

Cues

- Wiggle like a dolphin.
- Use big arms.
- Use straight arms.
- Take a quick breath.
- Have floppy ankles.
- Keep feet together.
- Kick twice.

Differentiation

- Move a licorice strand horizontally up and down to demonstrate the ribboning, or undulation, of the body for students to feel and see.
- Discuss the arching rainbow movement of a dolphin and have the student practice that movement over and under lane lines.
- Use physical guidance to move the arms in the correct fashion.
- Call out cues as the student is swimming.
- Have the student practice in shallow water so she can rest between practice trials.

How Far Can You Go?

Skill 6.13—Perform the Butterfly Stroke Progression 10 Times

Equipment

None

Preparation

None

Formation

The student is in the water at one end of the pool. The instructor is beside her.

Instructor Directions

Demonstrate 10 butterfly arm strokes while walking in the pool. Then have the student do the same.

Student Directions

The student walks while performing 10 butterfly arm strokes using rhythmic breathing.

Dolphin Dives

Skill 6.13—Perform the Butterfly Stroke Progression 10 Times

Equipment
Ten submersible objects that are motivating to the student, fins (optional)

Preparation
Place submersible objects underwater every 5 to 10 feet for the length of the pool.

Formation
The student is in the shallow end of the pool with his back to the wall and the instructor is standing next to the student.

Instructor Directions
Demonstrate the following dolphin dive 10 times: push off the bottom of the pool, spring into the air like a dolphin with your arms above your head in a streamlined position, catch a breath, and then enter the water hands first and submerge to the bottom of the pool in an arc like a rainbow, taking one dolphin kick. Although going all the way to the bottom of the pool is an exaggerated movement, it helps the student understand the concept of body undulation for the butterfly stroke. Now invite the student to do 10 dolphin dives, bring up an object on each dive, and hand it to you.

Student Directions
The student performs 10 dolphin dives to the bottom of the pool and picks up one object on each dive, handing it to you.

Ready, Set, Goose

Skill 6.14—Butterfly With Fins 12 Yards

Equipment
Fins

Preparation
Have the student put on fins (help if necessary).

Formation
The student is in the water on the side of the pool (facing across the width of the pool), wearing fins.

Instructor Directions
Explain that the student is to swim the width of the pool (12 yards) using the butterfly stroke only once you've said "Ready, set, go!" Then call out "Ready, set . . . " and finish with a word that is close to the word *go*, to fool the student (e.g. *Ready, set, goose* or *Ready, set, ghost*). Finally, say "Ready, set, go" to cue the student to begin her swim across the pool.

Student Directions

When you say "Ready, set, go!" the student performs the butterfly stroke for 12 yards with fins on.

Caterpillar, Caterpillar, Butterfly

Skill 6.15—Butterfly 25 Yards

Equipment

None

Preparation

At least three students are needed for this game.

Formation

One person is the tagger with a pool noodle and will walk back and forth on the pool deck near the students in the water. The other students are in the water holding the pool gutter or edge with one hand and ready to swim on the cue.

Instructor Directions

Explain that the tagger will walk back and forth, tapping swimmers and saying "Caterpillar." When he tags another student and says "Butterfly," that swimmer has a three-second lead in a 25-yard butterfly race to the other end of the pool. Have the students begin the game and observe and provide feedback when necessary.

Student Directions

Students wait in the water keeping one hand on the wall while the tagger taps their hands and says "Caterpillar." The students race when the tagger taps a student and says "Butterfly." That student has a three-second lead in the race.

Answer This

Skill 6.15—Butterfly 25 Yards

Equipment

None

Preparation

Come up with several current event questions appropriate to the students' age. Including several students makes this game more fun.

Formation

Students are in the pool with one hand holding the gutter or pool edge.

Instructor Directions

Explain that you will ask students a question, then say "Go." While the students are swimming the butterfly to the other end of the pool, they should be thinking of the answer. When they get to the other end, they shout out the answer as they touch the wall. Whoever gets the answer right gets to ask the next question after the instructor provides feedback to improve the strokes.

Student Directions

Students listen to your question and swim the butterfly stroke to the other end of the pool. Once there, they will shout out answers and receive feedback from the instructor to correct their stroke on the next lap. The first student to get the answer correct gets to ask the next question.

Individual Medley

The individual medley (IM) is a competitive event in which people swim all four competitive strokes for a predetermined distance (between 25 and 100 yards each) in this sequence: butterfly, backstroke, breaststroke, front crawl.

Cues

- Butter, back, breast, free (front crawl).
- Stretch it out during your stroke.
- Two-hand touch on the fly and breaststroke.
- Finish strong.

Differentiation

- Have cue cards at each end of the pool for those who need reminders of what stroke is next.
- Walk next to the lane near the wall and provide verbal cues for better strokes.

Prep for the IM

Skill 6.16—Swim the Individual Medley 100 Yards

Equipment

Stopwatch (optional)

Preparation

Arrange students in teams of four and give each student the name of one stroke they will do in the IM.

Formation

Students performing the butterfly and breaststroke are at one end of the pool, while students performing backstroke and front crawl are at the other end of the pool.

Instructor Directions

Explain to the students that they are going to do the sequence of the individual medley, but each of them will only swim one lap using one of the strokes, whereas in a real IM, one person does all four strokes. The student who is doing the butterfly stroke starts and then taps the swimmer on the other end, who then does the backstroke and then taps the swimmer who is going to do the breaststroke, who then swims to the other end and taps the swimmer doing the front crawl (freestyle). Once they are done, they can get out of the pool and discuss their strokes with you.

Student Directions

Students are going to do the sequence of the individual medley, but each of them will only swim one lap of one stroke instead of doing all four strokes as in a real IM. The swimmer who is doing butterfly stroke taps the swimmer on the other end, who then does the backstroke and taps the swimmer who is going to do the breaststroke, who then swims to the other end and taps the swimmer doing the front crawl (freestyle). Once they are done, they can get out of the pool and discuss their strokes with you.

Olympic IM

Skill 6.16—Swim the Individual Medley 100 Yards

Equipment

Air horn, stopwatch (optional)

Preparation

None

Formation

The swimmer is in the water with one hand on the wall

Instructor Directions

Explain the IM, give the command "Swimmers, take your mark," and then sound the air horn. Observe the swimmers, providing feedback when necessary. Keeping track of their splits (time that it takes the students to complete each lap) for each stroke will help you provide good feedback.

Student Directions

Students will swim all four competition strokes, for 25 yards each, with the appropriate turns between them. The butterfly swimmer uses the butterfly turn, the breaststroke swimmer uses the breaststroke turn, the backstroke swimmer uses the backstroke turn, and the front crawl swimmer uses the front flip turn.

References and Resources

American Red Cross. (2009). *Swimming and water safety*. Yardley, PA: Stay Well.

Asher, K.N., Rivara, F.P., Felix, D., Vance, L., & Dunne, R. (1995). Water safety training as a potential means of reducing risk of young children's drowning. *Injury Prevention*, *1* (4), 228-233.

Brenner, R.A., Taneja, G.S., Haynie, D.L., Trumble, A.C., Qian, C., Klinger, R.M., & Klevanoff, M.A. (2009). Association between swimming lessons and drowning in childhood: A case-control study. *Archives of Pediatrics & Adolescent Medicine*, *163* (3), 203-210.

Center for Universal Design. 1997. The principles of universal design. Retrieved July 14, 2012, from www.ncsu.edu/www/ncsu/design/sod5/cud/about_ud/udprinciplestext .htm

Centers for Disease Control and Prevention. (2012a). Drowning and prevention. Retrieved May 28, 2012, from www.cdc.gov/Features/DrowningPrevention/

Centers for Disease Control and Prevention. (2012b). Health benefits of water-based exercise. Retrieved February 24, 2012, from www.cdc.gov/healthywater/swimming/ health_benefits_water_exercise.html

Centers for Disease Control and Prevention. (2012c). Unintentional drowning: Get the facts. Retrieved June 26, 2012, from www.cdc.gov/homeandrecreationalsafety/water-safety/waterinjuries-factsheet.html

Chase N.L, Sui, X., & Blair, S.N. (2008). Swimming and all-cause mortality risk compared with running, walking, and sedentary habits in men. *International Journal of Aquatic Research and Education*, *2* (3), 213-223.

Columna, L. (2011). Assessing aquatics. In L.J. Lieberman & E.M. Kowalski (Eds.), *Assessment for everyone*. Reston, VA: National Association for Sport and Physical Education.

Columna, L., & Lieberman, L.J. (2011). *Overcoming language barriers through physical education: Using sign language and Spanish to engage everyone!* Champaign, IL: Human Kinetics.

Conatser, P., Block, M., & Lepore, M. (2000). Aquatic instructors' attitudes toward teaching students with disabilities. *Adapted Physical Activity Quarterly*, *17* (2), 197-207.

Ellis, M.K., Lieberman, L.J., & LeRoux, D. (2009). Using differentiated instruction in physical education. *Palaestra*, *24* (4), 19-23.

Gilchrist, J., Sacks, J.J., & Branche, C.M. (2000). Self-reported swimming ability in U.S. adults. *Public Health Reports*, *115* (2–3), 110-111.

Grosse, S. (2005). *Water learning*. Champaign, IL: Human Kinetics.

Hall, T., Strangman, N., & Meyer, A. (2003). *Differentiated instruction and implications for UDL implementation*. Wakefield, MA: National Center on Accessing the General Curriculum. Retrieved August 20, 2006, from www.cast.org/publications/ncac/ ncac_diffinstructudl.html

Halliwick Association of Swimming Therapy. (2002). The ten point programme. Halliwick AST. Retrieved August 15, 2012, from www.halliwick.org.uk/html/tenpoint.htm

Huettig, C., & Darden-Melton, B. (2004). Acquisition of aquatic skills by children with autism. *Palaestra*, *20* (2), 20-27.

Individuals with Disabilities Education Improvement Act. (2004). Pub. L. No. 108-446, 118 Stat. 2647 *et seq.*

Irwin, C.C., Irwin, R.L., & Ryan, T.D. (2009). Urban minority youth swimming (in) ability in the United States and associated demographic characteristics: Toward a drowning prevention plan. *Injury Prevention, 15,* 234-239.

Langendorfer, S.J., & Bruya, L.D. (1995). *Aquatic readiness: Developing water competence in young children.* Champaign, IL: Human Kinetics.

Lepore, M., Gayle, G.W., & Stevens, S.F. (2007). *Adapted aquatics programming: A professional guide.* Champaign, IL: Human Kinetics.

Lieberman, L.J., Lytle, R.K., & Clarcq, J.A. (2008). Getting it right from the start: Employing the universal design for learning approach to your curriculum. *Journal of Physical Education, Recreation, and Dance, 79* (2), 32-39.

Mace, R. (1998, June 19). A perspective on universal design. Presented at Designing for the 21st Century: An International Conference on Universal Design, Hofstra University, Hempstead, NY. Title and text edited by Jan Reagan, www.ncsu.edu/www/ncsu/design/sod5/cud/about_us/usronmacespeech.htm

McGuire, J., Scott, S., & Shaw, S. (2006). Universal design and its application in educational environments. *Remedial and Special Education, 27,* 166-175.

National Center on Universal Design for Learning. (2012). UDL guidelines—version 2.0. Retrieved August 4, 2012, from www.udlcenter.org/aboutudl/udlguidelines

National Institutes of Health. (2009). Swimming lessons do not increase drowning risk in young children. Retrieved June 26, 2012, from www.nih.gov/news/health/mar2009/nichd-02a.htm

Ortiz-Stuhr, E., & Columna, L. (2013). Aquatics. In S. Kasser & R. Lyttle (Eds.), *Inclusive physical activity: Promoting health for a lifetime* (2nd ed., pp. 217-227). Champaign, IL: Human Kinetics.

Rose, D., & Meyer, A. (2002). Teaching every student in the digital age: Universal design for learning. Alexandria, VA: Association for Supervision and Curriculum Development (ASCD).

Sports & Fitness Industry Association. (2011). 2011 Sports, Fitness & Recreational Activities Topline Participation Report. Retrieved June 26, 2012, from www.sgma.com/reports/276_2011-SPORTS,-FITNESS-AND-RECREATIONAL-ACTIVITIES-TOPLINE-PARTICIPATION-REPORT----NEW-RELEASE

Tomlinson, C.A. (1999a). Mapping a route toward differentiated instruction. *Educational Leadership, 57* (1), 12-16.

Tomlinson, C.A. (1999b). *The differentiated classroom: Responding to the needs of all learners.* Alexandria, VA: Association for Supervision and Curriculum Development (ASCD).

Tomlinson, C.A. (2001). *How to differentiate instruction in mixed-ability classrooms* (2nd ed.). Alexandria, VA: Association for Supervision and Curriculum Development (ASCD).

Tomlinson, C.A. (2011). Assessment and differentiation. Memphis, TN: ASCD Professional Development Institute. Retrieved June 26, 2012, from http://caroltomlinson.com/Presentations/2011ASCD_PDI_Memphis.pdf

U.S. Census Bureau. (2010). 2010 statistical abstract of the United States. Recreation and leisure activities: Participation in selected sports activities. Retrieved February 11, 2014, from www.census.gov/compendia/statab/2012/tables/12s1240.pdf

World Health Organization. (2012). Drowning. Retrieved August 15, 2012, from www.who.int/mediacentre/factsheets/fs347/en/index.html

Yang, L., Nong, Q.Q., Li, C., Feng, Q.M., & Lo, S.K. (2007). Risk factors for childhood drowning in rural regions of a developing country: A case-control study. *Injury Prevention, 13* (3), 178-182.

About the Authors

Monica Lepore, EdD, is a professor at West Chester University in West Chester, Pennsylvania. A master teacher of adapted aquatics, Dr. Lepore has been an American Red Cross water safety instructor for more than 25 years. She has a degree in leadership in adapted physical education and received the International Swimming Hall of Fame Adapted Aquatics Award in 2001. In 2006 she was named AAHPERD/AAPAR Adapted Physical Education Professional of the Year, and she has been on the Top 100 Aquatics Professionals list twice. She was chair of AAHPERD/AAPAR adapted aquatics from 2000 to 2005 and received a Meritorious Award from the Aquatic Council of AAHPERD/AAPAR in 2005. In her leisure time, Dr. Lepore enjoys swimming, biking, and hiking.

Luis Columna, PhD, is an associate professor in the exercise science and physical education department at Syracuse University. He holds three degrees in adapted physical education and physical education and has been engaged in teaching and scholarship in higher education for the past decade. His background includes teaching physical education in Puerto Rico and adapted physical education in the Denton, Texas, public schools. His research focuses on ways to increase the participation of families of children with disabilities in physical activity. He also studies methods to better prepare teachers to work with diverse populations, including children and their families. At the national level, Dr. Columna has served on numerous committees in several organizations. He was the chairperson for the Adapted Physical Activity Council for SHAPE America (formerly AAHPERD). Columna has given more than 100 workshops and presentations at the international, national, and state levels. He has authored numerous peer-reviewed articles for journals such as *Journal of Physical Education, Recreation and Dance; Journal of Teaching Physical Education;* and *Adapted Physical Activity Quarterly*. His hobbies include dancing, varied outdoor activities, and travel.

Lauren Friedlander Litzner, MS, is a health and physical education teacher in Montgomery County, Maryland. She earned a bachelor's degree from SUNY Cortland in physical education with a concentration in adapted physical education. She has a master's degree in community youth sport development from University of North Carolina at Greensboro. She has a master's from McDaniel College in physical education with a concentration in athletic administration. During her time in Cortland, Lauren earned the Major of the Year award through AAHPERD as well as Division III All-American status. She has taught nonswimmers and beginning swimmers at UNC Greensboro. She is currently teaching physical education at Piney Branch Elementary School, where she teaches swimming to students in third through fifth grade. Lauren has been a Red Cross water safety instructor since 2010 and is a member of SHAPE America and the Aerobics and Fitness Association of America. She is also a certified adapted aquatics instructor. Lauren enjoys swimming, playing tennis, teaching, and competing in triathlons.